Pink Ribbons, Inc.

Pink Ribbons, Inc.

Breast Cancer and the Politics
of Philanthropy

SAMANTHA KING

University of Minnesota Press
Minneapolis
London

Chapter 1 was first published as "An All-Consuming Cause: Breast Cancer, Corporate Philanthropy, and the Market for Generosity," *Social Text* 19, no. 4 (Winter 2001): 115–43; copyright Duke University Press; all rights reserved; reprinted by permission of Duke University Press. Chapter 2 was first published as "Doing Good by Running Well: Breast Cancer, the Race for the Cure, and New Technologies of Ethical Citizenship," in *Foucault, Cultural Studies, and Governmentality,* edited by Jack C. Bratich, Jeremy Packer, and Cameron McCarthy (Albany: SUNY Press, 2003), 295–316; reprinted with permission from SUNY Press. Parts of chapters 2 and 3 were previously published in "Pink Ribbons, Inc.: Breast Cancer Activism and the Politics of Philanthropy," *International Journal of Qualitative Studies in Education* 17, no. 4 (July–August 2004): 473–92; reprinted with permission of Taylor and Francis Group, http://www.tandf.co.uk. An earlier version of chapter 4 was first published as "Marketing Generosity: Avon Women's Health Programs and New Trends in Global Community Relations," *International Journal of Sports Marketing and Sponsorship* 3, no. 3 (September/October 2001): 267–90; reprinted courtesy of *International Journal of Sports Marketing and Sponsorship*; copyright International Marketing Reports, Ltd. Chapter 4 also appeared as "Marketing Generosity: The Avon Worldwide Fund for Women's Health and the Reinvention of Global Corporate Citizenship," in *Sport and Corporate Nationalisms,* edited by Michael L. Silk, David L. Andrews, and C. L. Cole (New York: Berg Publishers, 2005), 83–108.

Published by the University of Minnesota Press
111 Third Avenue South, Suite 290
Minneapolis, MN 55401-2520
http://www.upress.umn.edu

Library of Congress Cataloging-in-Publication Data

King, Samantha, 1970–
    Pink ribbons, inc. : breast cancer and the politics of philanthropy / Samantha King.
      p. cm.
    Includes bibliographical references and index.
    ISBN-13: 978-0-8166-4898-6 (hc/j : alk. paper)
    ISBN-10: 0-8166-4898-0 (hc/j : alk. paper)
    1. Breast—Cancer—Treatment—United States—Endowments. 2. Breast—Cancer—Treatment—United States—Finance. 3. Breast—Cancer—Patients—United States.
    I. Title.
    RC280.B8K56 2006
    362.196'99449—dc22

                                      2006013106

Printed in the United States of America on acid-free paper

The University of Minnesota is an equal-opportunity educator and employer.

12 11 10 09 08 07 06   10 9 8 7 6 5 4 3 2 1

Contents

Introduction

Breast Cancer and the Culture of Giving

On December 22, 1996, the *New York Times Magazine* ran a cover story declaring breast cancer "This Year's Hot Charity."[1] The backdrop to the boldly printed headline featured a head-and-shoulders shot of supermodel Linda Evangelista, slim, tanned, and naked. Evangelista was pictured with her left arm drawn across her chest, resting lightly—and provocatively—on her barely visible breasts. While the more controversial suggestion that breast cancer had become "sexy" was left to reside in the photograph of Evangelista, the written text addressed the recent ascendance of the disease to the pinnacle of charitable causes. Contributing writer Lisa Belkin argued that the valence of breast cancer as an issue could be attributed to a handful of passionate activists and their persistent networking among the wealthy and the powerful; the culturally appealing link between breast cancer, femininity, and nurturing; the willingness of corporations and politicians to embrace the cause; and the organizing experience gained by baby boomers who were active in the women's movements of the 1960s and 1970s. The piece focused particularly on Nancy Brinker, founder of the Susan G. Komen Breast Cancer Foundation, who is widely credited with turning the disease into a marketable product with which consumers, corporations, and politicians are eager to associate.

Just over three years previously, the magazine had run another cover story on the disease. This time the headline read, "You Can't Look Away Anymore: The Anguished Politics of Breast Cancer," and the accompanying image was a self-portrait of breast cancer activist and artist Matuschka with one side of her long white dress cut away to expose a mastectomy scar where her right breast had been.[2] The story focused on the rapid rise and notable success of the National Breast Cancer Coalition (NBCC), a Washington, D.C.–based feminist lobbying organization founded in 1991. The article detailed the agenda of the NBCC and the breast cancer movement more

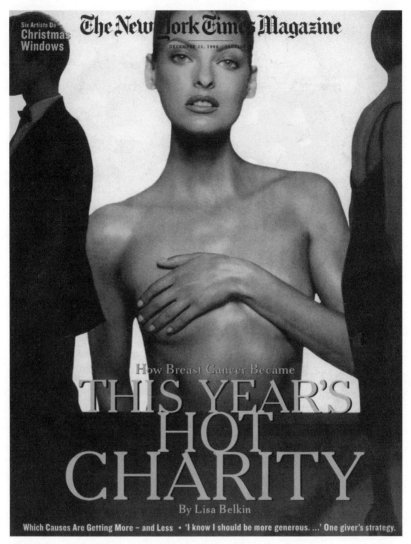

Cover of the New York Times Magazine, *December 22, 1996.*

broadly in terms of raising public awareness of the disease, seeking greater scientific and governmental attention to prevention, expanding the federal budget for research, and increasing the influence of breast cancer survivors over the federal research agenda.

Thus, in four short years, on the pages of one of the nation's most widely circulated magazines, breast cancer was reconfigured from a site of "Anguished Politics" to "This Year's Hot Charity." In 1993, the public

Cover of the New York Times Magazine, *August 15, 1993.*

was asked to think about the fight against the disease as a project of collective, grassroots activism that had made big strides in increasing funding for research and in winning a place for activist-survivors at the policy and research tables. In 1997, they were asked to think about this fight as an undertaking of wealthy individuals, CEOs, and politicians who had succeeded in making breast cancer chic.

The images through which the disease was made visible were also transformed: Matuschka's mutilated, though highly "stylized," chest, the result of an unnecessary mastectomy performed by an overzealous surgeon, replaced by the hypernormal femininity of Linda Evangelista's modestly covered yet perfectly intact breasts. Although both images were deployed to illustrate stories that focused almost exclusively on mainstream breast cancer activism and the interests of white, middle-class, professional women—a dominant feature of discourse on breast cancer, as we shall see—the move from Matuschka to Linda Evangelista corresponds to a clear change in how breast cancer is conceptualized in the realm of the popular.

The shift from politics to charity in the pages of the *New York Times Magazine* is but one instance in the ongoing cultural transformation of breast cancer in the United States since the early 1990s, a transformation that forms the focus of this book. In the pages that follow I trace how breast cancer has been reconfigured from a stigmatized disease and individual tragedy best dealt with privately and in isolation, to a neglected epidemic worthy of public debate and political organizing, to an enriching and affirming experience during which women with breast cancer are rarely "patients" and mostly "survivors." In the latter of these three configurations, the figure of the breast cancer survivor emerges as a beacon of hope who, through her courage and vitality, has elicited an outpouring of "American" generosity—a continued supply of which, we are led to believe, will ensure that the fight against the disease remains an unqualified success.

While on occasion this discourse of optimism references women who have died of breast cancer, less buoyant and more critical perspectives on progress in the struggle are now few and far between. This does not mean that the conceptualization of breast cancer as a political issue has dropped out of public circulation or that residual discourses of stigmatization have been entirely displaced. Rather, *Pink Ribbons, Inc.* shows how personal strength and optimism on the part of breast cancer survivors, alongside the research money that is generated by institutions and practices of consumer-oriented philanthropy, are now framed as the most effective tools for fighting the battle against the disease. This in turn has profound implications for how breast cancer is experienced by those who have the disease, how it is approached by the biomedical community who research and treat it, and how it is understood in the culture as a whole.

The emergence of breast cancer as a philanthropic cause par excellence tells a story about American culture that far exceeds any immediate association with the disease, however. The individualist orientation of much breast cancer activism must be understood, for instance, within the context of the powerful antifeminist backlash that characterized the 1980s and 1990s and which, among other consequences, had the effect of stifling more radical political discourses and encouraging women-centered social movements to distance themselves from explicitly feminist agendas. Moreover, as Verta Taylor and Marieke Van Willigen argue in their essay "Women's Self-Help and the Reconstruction of Gender: The Postpartum Support and Breast Cancer Movements," the emergence of an enormously popular self-help movement during the same period created an environment much more conducive to struggles geared toward internal reflection and transformation than toward external or structural change.[3]

While the shifting terrain of feminist politics in the last two decades of the twentieth century has been quite thoroughly researched, the same cannot be said of an equally important context for understanding the trajectory of the breast cancer movement; that is, the reinvigorated interest in organized giving that emerged within American society during the same period. A primary concern of *Pink Ribbons, Inc.* is thus to dissect the emergence of the current preoccupation with consumer-oriented philanthropic solutions to social problems, examine the concomitant appearance of a plethora of new techniques of soliciting corporate and individual donations of time and money, and analyze the explosion of discourse on the subject of charity. Although the argument presented here reveals that these developments have not escaped meaningful contestation and resistance, in *Pink Ribbons, Inc.* I argue that, overall, they have helped fashion a far-reaching constriction of public life, of the meaning of citizenship and political action, and of notions of responsibility and generosity. At the same time, these shifts have played a crucial role in the emergence of a reconfigured "neoliberal" state formation in which boundaries between the state and the corporate world are increasingly blurred as each elaborates the interests of the other, often at dispersed sites throughout the social body and through practices that misleadingly appear to be outside the realms of government or consumer capitalism.

I use the term "American generosity" to signify how, in contrast to other practices of citizenship (political protest or the paying of taxes, for instance), contemporary discourse on philanthropy and volunteerism posits charitable giving as an innate, timeless, and transhistorical trait that is distinctively "American." Americans give more than any other of the world's people, the national narrative goes, and they have done so "from the beginning." Wording from the Independent Sector, a nonprofit leadership forum, illustrates this point well: "America," it claims, "is a nation of volunteers and contributors, from the first public libraries and volunteer fire companies begun by Benjamin Franklin to those compassionate souls who joined Clara Barton's new Red Cross in the 1860s."[4] While this discourse appeals to a past in which citizens are imagined to have had more personal, localized, and moral bonds with their "communities," it has also emerged, in part, as a response to the public's desire for an ethical, meaningful, community-oriented life. By constituting well-intentioned consumption, personal generosity, and allegiance to a homogenized and privatized way of life as the normative configuration of citizenship, however, we shall see how the discourse of American generosity operates as yet another yardstick against which the capacities of individuals to become proper Americans is measured.

The Breast Cancer Movement in the United States

There has been a proliferation of academic and popular writing on the emergence of the breast cancer movement in the United States since the early 1990s.[5] This work has been crucial to our understanding of the relationship between breast cancer activism and the changing medical management of the disease, the policy changes and increased research funding that have been won as a result of the movement's activities, and the more open attitude toward the disease that it has helped engender. Although my central concern is with the "philanthropic arm" of the breast cancer movement and the broader culture of giving it has helped shape, one of my main contentions is that, for better or worse, the history of the movement as a whole, and its successes and failures, cannot be understood apart from the corporate-driven, consumer-oriented philanthropic culture that emerged in conjunction with it.

Here, then, I explore the history of the movement as it has been told by writers who have been justifiably committed to documenting the resistive strategies of grassroots activism and charting significant changes in biomedical and governmental approaches to breast cancer, rather than making what the National Breast Cancer Coalition calls "pink ribbon" activism, policy, and legislation a key focus of their work. What follows is not a comprehensive history but a necessarily skeletal engagement with some of the defining features of the movement. Many of the themes that emerge here will be revisited, albeit through an alternative lens, in the course of the book.

As far back as the 1930s, large numbers of women were involved in organized activities devoted to combating breast cancer. In 1936, the American

Society for the Control of Cancer (later to become the American Cancer Society) had formed the Women's Field Army (WFA), into which thousands of white, middle-class women were enlisted to deliver a message of early detection to others like them through media campaigns, leafleting, public lectures, and exhibitions. This was not a grassroots or feminist mobilization but rather a strategy devised by powerful male physicians to be carried out by unpaid workers who were eager to be active in the public sphere but were prevented from entering the waged labor force.[6] As we shall see, seventy years later, the WFA's focus on early detection and treatment and its reliance on traditional gender relations, in which wives and mothers were designated as responsible for the health of themselves, their families, and their communities, continue to characterize the mainstream of breast cancer activism in the United States.

This is not to suggest that this model has gone unchallenged: the development of the women's health movement in the 1970s and its critique of the patriarchal and paternalistic nature of medical practice also laid important groundwork for the specific issues that breast cancer activists would address in the decades to come. Although, as Ellen Leopold writes, breast cancer was not a central issue for this first generation of women's health campaigners, whose energy was largely devoted to the fight for reproductive freedoms, the feminist notion of women's "right to choose" in all decisions affecting their health became "deeply engrained in the culture" and has "to varying degrees, underwritten almost all subsequent women's health campaigns."[7] Indeed, it was in this historical context that several famous women—Shirley Temple Black (1973), Betty Ford (1974), and Happy Rockefeller (1974)—decided to break with tradition and speak publicly about their breast cancer diagnoses. Although none of these women professed a political agenda in relation to their illness or sought to challenge the medical status quo, their announcements were inevitably informed by the change in public attitudes toward women's health and bodily autonomy that second-wave feminism had provoked.[8] Moreover, the effect of their decisions was profoundly important in moving breast cancer out of the realm of secrecy and into the public domain. The extensive media coverage that followed Betty Ford's diagnosis, in particular—including uncommonly detailed and explicit discussions of the etiology of breast cancer, methods of detection, treatment options, and the psychological impact of losing a breast—resulted in an upsurge in breast examinations and mammography and provided a crucial boost to the process of destigmatization.[9]

The publication in 1975 of Rose Kushner's *Breast Cancer: A Personal History and Investigative Report,* in which the author criticized the practice of performing one-step mastectomies without the consent of the patient, in addition to a range of other highly problematic medical practices, is also widely acknowledged as a turning point in the history of the disease.[10] Although Kushner was not the first woman to write about her personal experience with breast cancer, her work was unique in its attempt to connect her experience to that of other women and thus to transform the disease from a personal problem into a social issue. In Leopold's words:

> Kushner's willingness to tackle so many of the obstacles she had encountered herself, and her ability to bring the public's attention to them, laid the groundwork for what eventually would become the modern culture of breast cancer. At its most basic, this was the recognition that the disease had a continuous presence within the culture, independent of its victims. Breast cancer was no longer viewed as a string of isolated events, surfacing for a moment each time the news of a friend or relative's death was passed on and then scurrying back to its hiding place. It now began to acquire staying power, a kind of cultural depth.[11]

Kushner's exposé prompted a decade of nationwide campaigning for informed consent legislation at the state level, and as activist and advocacy groups sprang up around the country, something like a national movement began to emerge.

Maren Klawiter's account of this history, "Reshaping the Contours of Breast Cancer: From Private Stigma to Public Actions," is among the most compelling.[12] She makes visible the connections between changes in the medical management of breast cancer, the destigmatization of the disease, and the growth of activism. She shows how a multiplication of treatment regimens, a proliferation of support groups, and the expansion of screening into asymptomatic populations during the 1980s and 1990s helped produce new social spaces, solidarities, and sensibilities among breast cancer survivors and activists. In other words, she points to the ways in which changes in the treatment of women by the medical profession, changes that were themselves preceded by the fledgling activism of women such as Rose Kushner, opened up numerous spaces in which they could talk openly about their experiences of the disease with one another, thus enabling the emergence of a multifaceted breast cancer movement.

One of the first formal indications of the scope of the movement materialized in 1986 with the formation of the National Alliance of Breast Cancer

Organizations (NABCO).[13] Run by Amy Langer, the aim of NABCO was to provide resources for breast cancer patients and "women at risk." The interest in a national umbrella organization such as this was made clear by the fact that only eight years into its existence NABCO comprised more than 350 member organizations. As Karen Stabiner writes in her account of the movement, *To Dance with the Devil: The New War on Breast Cancer,* "Women depended on NABCO for everything from information on clinical trials to advice on where to buy a wig."[14] Still missing, however, was a more activist-oriented national organization that would challenge the federal research agenda, much as the AIDS movement was doing at that time. NABCO, which over the years became almost entirely funded by the pharmaceutical industry and had a membership consisting mostly of members of the health care industry, was not in a position to lead this charge.

The need for such a body had become clearer than ever in the last three years of George H. W. Bush's presidency (1989–92). During this time an intense struggle had taken place over the introduction of Medicare coverage for mammography, with a provision being passed, then overturned, and then finally restored after a revolt by a number of Congresswomen against their own Republican leadership. In response to growing frustration among breast cancer advocates within and outside the government, Bush had established a nonpartisan President's Commission on Breast Cancer in 1991, chaired by Nancy Brinker of the increasingly influential Susan G. Komen Breast Cancer Foundation. When Bush failed to support legislation transferring $210 million in defense spending to breast cancer research the following year, however, breast cancer became an issue in the presidential campaign, and advocates such as Gloria Steinem and Representative Patricia Schroeder campaigned on behalf of candidate Bill Clinton on this very issue.

It was during this period of heightened awareness that the National Breast Cancer Coalition (NBCC) was created, with the purpose of influencing government policy on the disease. The NBCC was the brainchild of well-known breast cancer surgeon Dr. Susan Love and Susan Hester, a Washington, D.C., fund-raiser and director of the Mary-Helen Mautner Project for Lesbians with Cancer. From an initial meeting of seventy-five groups in 1991, including Breast Cancer Action of San Francisco and the Women's Community Cancer Project of Cambridge, the coalition grew to include three hundred affiliate organizations and came to exert a major influence on the direction of federal breast cancer policy in the 1990s.

An early sign of the organization's potential came in 1993 when, soon after his inauguration, President Bill Clinton met with a delegation from the NBCC and shortly thereafter announced that the Department of Health and Human Services, in partnership with breast cancer advocates, would develop a national action plan in response to the report of the Bush-appointed commission.[15] The commission's report, released in October 1993, recommended that the federal government spend at least $500 million a year on breast cancer research, called for improved coordination among researchers, recommended that legal standards for mammograms be adopted, and asked for an increase in programs to educate women on the need to undergo screening. In the years that followed the release of the report, an alliance between the federal government and private industry researchers to divert military and aerospace technology toward early breast cancer detection emerged; the Centers for Disease Control's (CDC) National Breast and Cervical Cancer Early Detection Program, which provides screening services for low-income and medically underserved women, was extended to all fifty states; Medicare coverage of mammograms was introduced; and further regulation of mammography quality and standards was initiated.

Perhaps the most easily measurable change brought about by the breast cancer movement over the past fourteen years, however, is in the amount of federal funding devoted to research. Following the NBCC's campaign to inundate members of Congress and the president with hundreds of thousands of letters during 1991 (according to Stabiner, Bush did not read them) and a second effort a year later (this time a petition drive), total government spending on research rose from $155 million in 1992 to $400 million in 1993.[16] National Cancer Institute (NCI) spending patterns were reflected in this overall increase such that by 1993, the NCI allocated more money for research on breast cancer than for prostate, ovarian, colorectal, and liver cancers combined.[17] The period between 2000 and 2005 saw a significant growth in funds devoted to prostate cancer, due in large part to the emergence of a prostate cancer movement that models itself explicitly on the breast cancer movement (although, as discussed in chapter 5, it often trades in antifeminist, anti-breast-cancer movement politics). The prostate cancer movement has also been able to capitalize on Lance Armstrong's high-profile battle with testicular cancer and his subsequent charitable crusade that had resulted in the sale of 55 million yellow "Livestrong" wristbands by March 2006. Armstrong dedicated the prostate cancer awareness stamp in May 1999, and his very public battle with testicular cancer has helped strengthen the profile of men's cancers in general. But breast cancer still receives far more NCI funding than any other cancer. Indeed by 2004, the NCI funding level for breast cancer was $566.2 million, with research for prostate cancer in second place at $308.5 million.[18]

Notwithstanding the optimistic character of mainstream discourse on the outcomes of breast cancer research, which relies heavily—and often uncritically—on the language of "progress," "breakthrough," and "cure," the extent to which this high level of funding has positively affected breast cancer incidence and mortality rates remains to be seen. For example, a woman's lifetime risk of breast cancer has increased from 1 in 22 in the 1940s to 1 in 7 in 2004.[19] Breast cancer incidence, in other words, rose steadily throughout the twentieth century, a trend that has continued on an annual basis since the 1980s. Indeed, according to the NCI Surveillance Epidemiology and End Results (SEER) data, the estimated annual percentage change for breast cancer is 2.1 percent, which means that breast cancer incidence rates are increasing at a rate of 2.1 percent each year. These figures translate into 212,930 new cases of invasive breast cancer among women in the United States in 2005, along with 58,490 new cases of in situ breast cancer.[20] There is much debate about how to explain the increase in incidence: while some parties, such as Breast Cancer Action, point to research on factors such as exposure to radiation and synthetic chemicals, others, including organizations such as the American Cancer Society and the National Cancer Institute, claim that it can be accounted for by the spread of screening and the introduction of technology that enables smaller cancers to be identified.[21]

Mortality rates have also been rising since World War II at least, and only recently have very small decreases in these rates occurred. According to NCI SEER data, the decrease in the U.S. breast cancer mortality rate was about 1.8 percent each year from 1989 to 1996. It is estimated that in 2005 there were a total of 40,870 deaths from the disease, 40,410 among women and 460 among men.[22] If these figures are broken down in order to consider differences among women, we find that women of color have persistently lower rates of screening and shorter survival after diagnosis. Although records show that since 1990 there has been a slight drop in mortality for women as a whole, the rates for American Indian and Alaskan Native women have risen slightly. Most striking is the divergence in long-term mortality trends between African American and white women. In

2000, there were 30 percent more excess deaths among African American women than among their white counterparts.[23]

Although research has shown that there are a variety of marked social inequalities across the "breast cancer continuum" (defined as risk, incidence, screening, diagnosis, treatment, survival, and mortality), the research has mostly focused on racial disparities between black women and white women, with less attention to other groups of women, to socioeconomic status, to the interaction of race with socioeconomic status, or to a range of other axes of difference such as disability and sexual identity. The research that does exist suggests that breast cancer across the continuum is related to socioeconomic status, although the relationship tends to vary by race, particularly in terms of incidence and diagnosis.[24] In other words, inequalities in women's experiences of breast cancer are consistent with health inequalities in general, so that even middle-class women of color face disparate treatment in comparison with their white, middle-class counterparts.

Breast cancer activists and biomedical practitioners in the more critical reaches of the movement argue that such disparities are in part a reflection of a historically entrenched concern with funding research rather than access to or payment for treatment.[25] This prejudice arises, they argue, because the cancer control establishment in general (i.e., the American Cancer Society and other large cancer organizations, the National Cancer Institute, the National Centers for Disease Control, the Food and Drug Administration, and pharmaceutical and biotech companies) and the breast cancer movement in particular have from their inception been composed of affluent individuals for whom the costs or availability of medical care are irrelevant.[26] It would also be safe to assume that an aversion to dealing with access to treatment grows out of a broader culture of for-profit health research and care and a commitment to maintaining market-driven service provision.

An issue that occupies a more prominent position in debates about financial support for breast cancer concerns the overwhelming preference among funding agencies (both nonprofit and for-profit) for research that focuses on screening and treatment rather than prevention. Although this situation has altered slightly as a result of activist efforts in the 1990s and a more general, if reluctant, recognition of the importance of preventive medicine, it is still the case that the vast majority of funding for breast cancer goes toward high-stakes screening and treatment-oriented research and, increasingly, genetic research, which is often misleadingly described as preventive. Barron Lerner's history of breast cancer diagnosis and treatment in the United States, *The Breast Cancer Wars: Hope, Fear, and the Pursuit of a Cure in Twentieth-Century America,* reveals that a focus on research oriented toward early detection and treatment (or "cure") emerged in the late-nineteenth century and has remained the dominant mode of approaching the disease ever since, even though the preferred methods of detection and treatment have varied within and between historical periods.[27] While the complex grid of forces that Lerner identifies as key to the emergence of the prevailing approach is beyond the scope of this book, suffice it to say that he provides ample evidence of the degree to which research on early detection and treatment has become entrenched. It is also the case, of course, that the clinical researchers, oncologists, drug companies, and equipment manufacturers at the heart of the cancer establishment have much to lose in terms of money and prestige if the tide were to turn away from the search for better therapies.

Philanthropy and the Breast Cancer Movement

Questions of how breast cancer became the top priority in cancer research and why the research agenda took the shape it did have been answered in part by the aforementioned analyses of the emergence of a well-organized and funded social movement. Understandably dedicated to documenting the oppositional strategies of grassroots activism and to charting substantive shifts in the funding and regulation of research, screening, and treatment, however, scholars of the breast cancer movement have not pursued a sustained analysis of what I call the "philanthropic arm" of the breast cancer movement or the (related) emergence of a culture of breast cancer survivorship.[28] Yet, as I have noted, fund-raising for breast cancer is one of the most visible and accessible of the available forms of public participation in the fight against the disease. Thus, although the headline of the 1996 *New York Times Magazine* article, "This Year's Hot Charity," implied that philanthropic interest in breast cancer was perhaps a fad that would soon diminish, this has not proven to be the case: more than one million people participated in the Susan G. Komen Breast Cancer Foundation's Race for the Cure events in 2005. Almost all the breast cancer nonprofits that have proliferated in the past two decades continue to thrive, and new organizations are formed all the time. Breast cancer research remains as a—if not *the*—favorite issue for corporations seeking to attract consumers through cause-related marketing campaigns. In 2005, for example, automaker Ford approached Grammy Award–winning rock star and breast cancer survivor Melissa Etheridge about recording a single that would serve as an "anthem for the fight against breast cancer."[29] The result, *I Run for Life,* was released that same year and is sold exclusively through the iTunes Music Store, with 80 percent of the download price going to the Komen Foundation and 20 percent going to the Dr. Susan Love Research Foundation. During National Breast Cancer Awareness Month in 2004, hundreds of buildings all over the United States, including the Empire State Building in New York, the St. Louis Arch, the Sears Tower in Chicago, and the Benjamin Franklin Bridge in Philadelphia, were illuminated by pink lights with the aim of building breast cancer "awareness." And all these developments continue to intersect with the creation of policy at the state and federal levels to encourage breast-cancer-related philanthropy among the public.

One possible reason for the omission of philanthropic organizations from existing analyses might be that they do not fit neatly into traditional sociological definitions of a social movement organization (the dominant theoretical framework employed in the literature on breast cancer activism) because they tend to be primarily concerned with fund-raising rather than collective action to bring about social change. However, all the large breast cancer foundations undertake some form of advocacy and education as they go about their fund-raising, and the diverse character of the work they undertake has played a pivotal role in reshaping the political and social context of the disease. It would be hard to deny, for instance, the impact of the Komen Foundation, and particularly the Race for the Cure, in reconfiguring popular attitudes toward women with breast cancer in the United States. Even if the shift from "victim" to "survivor" is fraught with problems, this discursive reconfiguration represents a change that came about in part because of collective action organized, albeit in a top-down manner, by the Komen Foundation.

In this vein, one of the central arguments of *Pink Ribbons, Inc.* is that breast cancer became the "biggest disease on the cultural map," in Barbara Ehrenreich's words, not simply because of effective political organizing during the 1980s and 1990s, but because of an informal alliance of large corporations (particularly pharmaceutical companies, mammography equipment manufacturers, and cosmetics producers), major cancer charities, the state, and the media that emerged at around the same time and was able to capitalize on growing public interest in the disease.[30] National Breast Cancer Awareness Month (NBCAM), founded in 1985 by Zeneca (now

AstraZeneca), a multinational pharmaceutical corporation and then subsidiary of Imperial Chemical Industries, is possibly the most highly visible and familiar manifestation of this alliance. AstraZeneca is the manufacturer of tamoxifen, the best-selling breast cancer drug, and until corporate reorganization in 2000 was under the auspices of Imperial Chemical, a leading producer of the carcinogenic herbicide acetochlor, as well as numerous chlorine and petroleum-based products that have been linked to breast cancer.

The aim of NBCAM from its inception has been to promote mammography as the most effective weapon in the fight against breast cancer. In 2006, the National Breast Cancer Awareness campaign was underwritten by a board of sponsors comprising fifteen organizations, including medical associations such as the American College of Radiology, breast cancer service organizations such as the Y-ME National Breast Cancer Organization, and government agencies such as the National Cancer Institute, "working in partnership to raise awareness and provide access to screening services."[31] AstraZeneca underwrites the cost of the promotional and educational materials that make up the "official" NBCAM campaign and has sole power of approval over any pamphlet, poster, or advertisement used by NBCAM. AstraZeneca's interest in promoting mammography and thereby raising detection rates and increasing sales of tamoxifen is a story widely circulated in activist circles and progressive media but almost entirely ignored in mainstream discourse. And, not surprisingly, AstraZeneca and its allies in National Breast Cancer Awareness Month, such as the American Cancer Society, continue to carefully avoid environmental issues, or indeed reference to prevention in general.

The success of AstraZeneca's campaign, as the analysis that follows reveals, is such that hundreds of organizations that are not official sponsors of NBCAM now also run breast cancer awareness promotions during October, almost always with the dual aim of promoting mammography and raising money. As such, NBCAM has taken on a life of its own and developed into a high-profile campaign for early detection ("awareness") and breast cancer charity produced by a disjointed but vast assemblage of players. Beyond the official partners in the project, these players include cable and network television; local and national magazines and newspapers; nonprofit organizations; federal, state, and local government agencies; health care educators and providers; pharmaceutical corporations; the cosmetic and fashion industries; and the world of professional sports. Moreover, this corporate-administered and corporate-financed campaign is now officially cosponsored by the Centers for Disease Control and Prevention and the National Cancer Institute and is recognized on an annual basis by the president of the United States in the form of an official proclamation. NBCAM propaganda has even found its way into fictional media content: as part of the Ford Motor Company's breast cancer campaign in 2005, the actresses who portray women doctors and nurses on NBC's *ER* were featured wearing limited-edition Ford Breast Cancer Awareness silk scarves, designed by Lilly Pulitzer, in advertisements titled "The Women of *ER* Get Tied to the Cause." In addition, *ER* featured a story line that dealt with breast cancer "awareness" in two October 2005 episodes. Not surprisingly, the shows included the promotion of mammography by following a nurse who is forced to confront the fact that she has never been screened despite a history of cancer in her family.[32]

My purpose in drawing attention to the ways that organizing around breast cancer has been conceptualized and the ways in which the work of the Komen Foundation or NBCAM have been largely excluded from the research is not simply to suggest that we need to add consideration of philanthropic groups and practices to existing analyses. Rather, it is to argue that an investigation of the role of organized giving, particularly consumer-oriented giving, in the politics of breast cancer requires that we rethink some key assumptions about the movement and the meaning of breast cancer in the contemporary United States. In this context, *Pink Ribbons, Inc.* seeks to offer an alternative mapping of the history of breast cancer and the multifaceted movement the disease has spawned, by showing how corporate marketing strategies, government policies, and the agendas of large nonprofits serve to reinforce one another in the social production of the disease.

I use the term *breast cancer culture*—and hope to retain the complex variety of meanings associated with the word *culture*—to describe the effects of this articulation.[33] In other words, my aim is to highlight those forms of breast-cancer-related social identification, affiliation, and organization that exist outside of the confines of social movement organizations or political action and change narrowly defined. But I am also interested in forms of collective experience that operate beyond medical institutions or the range of groups and organizations that provide screening, diagnosis, treatment, and therapy for people with breast cancer. Thus, the chapters that follow include ethnographic analyses of mass participation, physical-activity-based fund-raising events such as the Komen Foundation's Race for the Cure and the Avon Breast Cancer Walk. I consider the history of the immensely popular breast cancer fund-raising stamp as it is reproduced in the *Congressional Record* and other government and party political documents. In order to explore the emergence of an entire industry devoted to marketing products with a breast cancer theme, I explore business management literature on corporate philanthropy and cause-related marketing, print media and televisual promotional campaigns related to breast cancer, and annual reports and newsletters from breast cancer nonprofits.

In addition to the methodological diversity that attention to breast cancer as *culture* demands, a focus on the cultural dimensions of the disease allows me to highlight the distinct set of signs and symbols—style, even—now associated with it. The pink ribbon is the most ubiquitous of these symbols, its presence on a T-shirt, a billboard, or a Hallmark card conferring an instantly recognizable set of meanings and values related to femininity, charity, white middle-class womanhood, and survivorship. But it is also the case that a range of consumer items unmarked by a ribbon logo, from the pink "Cook for the Cure" KitchenAid mixer to the pink-and-white necklaces and bracelets frequently worn by survivors, are also now readily identified with the breast cancer cause.

Given the prominence of the pink ribbon in breast cancer culture and its centrality to the argument presented in the pages that follow, a brief detour through its history seems pertinent here. The most thorough chronicle of the emergence of the ribbon, authored by Sandy Fernandez, appeared in *MAMM* magazine in 1998.[34] (In the context of the ongoing cultural preoccupation with breast cancer, *MAMM* is itself an interesting example: launched in October 1997 by the publisher of *POZ* magazine for people living with and otherwise affected by the AIDS/HIV epidemic, it is the first glossy magazine devoted to breast and reproductive cancers.) Fernandez writes that the use of satin ribbons to connote messages of hope and inspiration is thought to have first occurred in 1979, when Penne Laingen, the wife of an American who had been taken hostage in Iran, tied yellow ribbons around the trees in her front yard.[35] The television news media picked up the story and soon people across the country were doing the same thing in order to signal their desire to see the safe return of the hostages.

Eleven years later, the activist art group Visual AIDS, seeking to gain broader cultural recognition of the devastating effects of HIV, took note of the yellow ribbons that were once again in vogue as the United States began its first Gulf war and decided to use the idea to draw attention to "our boys dying here at home." They settled on a bright red ribbon and persuaded actor Jeremy Irons to wear it to the nationally televised Tony awards event. As Marita Sturken writes in "AIDS as Kitsch":

> Soon red ribbons were turning up not only at AIDS events and art events but also on the street and at the mall, and designer red-ribbon glitter pins began to flood the market. In 1993 the U.S. Postal Service even issued a red-ribbon stamp promoting AIDS awareness. In terms of ubiquitousness and popularity, the red ribbon was an instant success.[36]

Sturken notes, however, that the moment the ribbon entered the public arena it became the site of a fierce debate over the mainstreaming of AIDS discourse and the normalizing of activism that detractors claimed accompanied the popularity of the ribbon. Such debates were also to occur in the breast cancer community and, in fact, continue to this day, with members in the more radical reaches of the movement refusing to don this particular symbol, preferring instead "Cancer Sucks!" pins and, importantly, the maintenance of an approach that refuses to see breast cancer as something pretty or pleasant.[37]

Soon after Irons's appearance, according to Fernandez, ribbons of every color imaginable were being designed by supporters of a host of charitable causes. They became so popular in such a short time, much like the silicone wristbands that flooded the philanthropic market in 2005, that the *New York Times* declared 1992 "The Year of the Ribbon."[38] It was not long, of course, before a breast cancer ribbon emerged. It is not surprising, given their commitment to breast cancer marketing, that the Susan J. Komen Breast Cancer Foundation was the first breast cancer organization to latch on to the idea by distributing pink ribbons to every participant in its New York City Race for the Cure (they also, later, tried unsuccessfully to trademark the ribbon). Around the same time, Charlotte Haley, a sixty-eight-year-old with a history of breast cancer in her family, began making peach-colored ribbons in her dining room at home. Each set of five came with a card that read: "The National Cancer Institute annual budget is $1.8 billion, only 5 percent goes for cancer prevention. Help us wake up our legislators and America by wearing this ribbon." A few months later, *Self* magazine, which was planning its second annual National Breast Cancer Awareness Month issue, with Evelyn Lauder, senior corporate vice president at Estée Lauder, as guest editor, decided to create a ribbon that would be distributed at the company's cosmetics counters across the country. At first, according to Fernandez, the magazine approached Haley asking her to work with them on the plan and, as part of the deal, relinquish the concept of the ribbon. Haley refused, claiming (correctly as it turns out) that she feared the commercialization of her approach, and so *Self,* in consultation with its lawyers, settled on a different color: pink.

In the fall of 1992, Estée Lauder makeup counters distributed 1.5 million ribbons, each accompanied by a card with instructions on how to perform a proper breast self-exam. They also collected more than 200,000 petitions urging the White House to push for increased funding for research. By the following year, according to Carol Cone, founder of Cone Communications and a major force in cause-related marketing in the United States, the Avon cosmetics company was also seeking to stake out a claim on breast cancer. "The challenge for Avon at the time was creating a unique program," Cone told Fernandez. There were already fifteen companies involved in breast cancer by that time, by Cone's accounting, and Avon settled on a pink ribbon, this time a piece of jewelry made of enamel and gold case. The brooch was a great success, and soon thereafter pink ribbons began to appear on products ranging from sneakers to food processors. Quite astonishingly, given the swiftness with which marketing trends come and go, the fad for pink ribbon products is alive and well in 2006 and shows no sign of abating.

While it would be easy to dismiss "pink ribbon" merchandise as a superficial and insignificant by-product of the upsurge in interest in the breast cancer cause, I prefer to approach it as a particularly prominent manifestation of the tight alliances that have formed between large breast cancer foundations and corporations, of the insidiously gendered nature of cause-related marketing that helps reproduce associations between women and shopping, and of a more general tendency to deploy consumption as a major avenue of political participation. In order to understand the reconfiguration of the meaning of breast cancer in U.S. culture, then, it is important to explore the upsurge in political organizing devoted to fighting the disease. But it is also necessary to examine, in conjunction, the broader social, economic, political, and cultural shifts that have prompted nonprofit consultants, corporate executives, marketers, politicians, and numerous other members of the American public to "latch on to" breast cancer as a favorite charitable cause. What, in other words, is the appeal of breast cancer? Or, more accurately, how and why has it been *made* to appeal?

Neoliberalism and the Politics of Philanthropy

It should be clear by now that the concerns of the book go beyond a focus on the politics of breast cancer. Indeed, at the broadest level, its aim is to consider how the consumption-based culture of organized giving that has grown up around the disease might facilitate our understanding of a more general preoccupation in the contemporary United States with philanthropic practice as a necessary feature of "proper" citizenship and "good" government. This preoccupation takes a variety of forms: In the post-welfare-reform era politicians frequently appeal to philanthropy and volunteerism as morally and economically viable solutions to newly created gaps in the social safety net. The mass media offer a constant flow of stories recounting the generosity of individual Americans, with the focus ranging from "ordinary" people striving to make a difference in their communities to the newest generation of billionaire philanthropists such as Ted Turner and Bill Gates. Corporate-sponsored employee volunteerism programs are now commonplace. Increasing numbers of commodities are sold to the public through their association with social causes. States across the union mandate volunteer service as a requirement for high school graduation. Satin ribbons and silicone wristbands of every color imaginable are worn to mark awareness of a myriad of issues ranging from breast cancer to "troop support." And Americans walk, run, swim, bike, and climb hundreds of thousands of miles each year to raise money for any number of charitable causes.

Although the United States has long been characterized by a strong voluntary, or nonprofit, sector with close ties to large corporations and prominent businesspeople, the deployment of philanthropic initiatives as central components of corporate marketing strategy, to take one example from the list, is a fairly recent development. *Pink Ribbons, Inc.* explores this and other shifts in relation to the rise of neoliberalism as the dominant organizing principle of government and the economy in the past quarter century. *Neoliberalism,* like any descriptor mobilized by a diverse range of actors to describe a complex set of forces, is a contested term. For the purposes of the argument that follows, I use it to refer to a philosophy and a set of economic and political policies aimed at cutting expenditures on public goods such as education, health care, and income assistance in order to enhance corporate profit rates. Under the auspices of bodies such as the International Monetary Fund, the World Bank, the U.S. Treasury, and the World Trade Organization, the most common strategies used to implement this goal include fiscal austerity, privatization, and deregulation. In Lisa Duggan's words, the general effect of this "wide-ranging political and cultural project" has been to encourage the dramatic "upward redistribution of a range of resources" and a widespread tolerance of increasing inequality in the context of a gradual elimination of a concept of the public good.[39]

Under this regime, public-private initiatives and individual and corporate giving are promoted as morally and economically viable means through which to respond to societal needs, in lieu of the state's role in mitigating the social effects of capitalism. In this context, we can see how George W. Bush's Armies of Compassion initiative, which allows government appropriations and tax benefits for church-based services, builds on the work done by the three previous administrations to substitute general tax collections with voluntary revenue enhancers and to devolve responsibility for functions previously administered by state agencies to individuals and non- and for-profit organizations.[40]

Through analyses of the development of corporate philanthropy programs with a breast cancer theme and federal government policies to encourage voluntary initiatives in support of breast cancer research, the book illustrates how business strategy and political ideology—and, for that matter, business ideology and political strategy—have interacted in the production of techniques designed to encourage private giving. Furthermore, it points to the ways in which participation in giving, of time or money, is viewed not simply as a preferable way to fund public services, but as a vehicle for instilling civic and self-responsibility in the American people, who are understood to have become apathetic and dependent citizens of a "nanny" state. Unlike the divisive and apathy-inducing technologies of welfare (in George H. W. Bush's words, "Government programs can erode the enthusiasm that volunteers should have—and do have—in their hearts"), donning a brightly colored silicone bracelet or participating in a leisurely 5K stroll on a Sunday afternoon is thought to help rekindle America's "traditional" culture of personal generosity and constitute a more harmonious, benevolent, personally responsible, and active citizenry.[41]

While citizenship responsibilities in this configuration are most frequently enacted through consumption, my analysis suggests that the ideal citizen is not, to quote Nikolas Rose, envisioned as "the isolated and selfish atom of the free market."[42] Instead, in the contemporary organization of political responsibility, subjects are addressed and understood as individuals who are responsible to themselves and for others in their "community."

Ideally, responsibility is not to be demonstrated by paying taxes to support social welfare programs or by expressing dissent and making political demands on behalf of one's fellow citizens. Instead, in the words of former president Bill Clinton, Americans must be taught that "to be a good citizen, in addition to going to work and going to school and paying your taxes and obeying the law, you have to be involved in community service."[43]

Thus, from Ronald Reagan's 1981 Task Force on Private Sector Initiatives, established to develop, support, and promote private sector leadership in community development and social service, to George H. W. Bush's Points of Light initiative, to Bill Clinton's 1997 President's Summit on America's Future held to solicit individual and corporate generosity as a "complement" to welfare reform legislation, to George W. Bush's faith-based initiatives, four successive federal administrations have sought to establish the organizational and subjective conditions through which to re-shape relations between the state and the individual. They have done this not simply by rolling back the public welfare system with the hope that the charitable impulses of citizens and corporations will flourish, but by helping to create techniques, strategies, and programs—frequently in partnership with nonprofit or business entities—aimed at producing volunteer and philanthropist citizens.

Despite the association between volunteerism and freedom in American culture and the pervasive view that the social state has stifled the innate generosity of the American people, the account that follows suggests that the turn toward volunteerism and philanthropy does not mark a radical turn away either from government or from the role of the state in governing, as the rhetoric of those who celebrate the "end of big government" suggests. Rather, I maintain that it marks a shift toward a different form of governing and the emergence of an alternatively constituted state. This is an argument that I develop through the course of the book, as I seek to highlight how government, or the "conduct of conduct," to use Michel Foucault's formulation, is dispersed throughout the social body, rather than resting solely or even primarily with the state. This is not to trivialize the role of the state in governing, particularly in a historical conjuncture that has seen an "intensification, acceleration, and integration of governing strategies under a state of emergency, or permanent war," but rather to show how functions that we might traditionally associate with the state, or connections between the governor and the governed, occur at innumerable decentered, dispersed, and often private or commercial sites within the social body.[44] The turn to volunteerism and philanthropy can thus be read as an effect of the desire to "govern at a distance" that theorists such as Nikolas Rose have identified as a central characteristic of neoliberal thought.[45] Institutions, programs, and techniques designed to encourage volunteerism and philanthropy, for example, are mechanisms of governance that have varying degrees of autonomization from the state. Nonetheless, these networks and techniques are frequently established through alliances with the state and, even when operating in deeply privatized settings (a National Football League advertising campaign, for example), often work to "elaborate core state interests."[46]

By focusing on the explosion of breast-cancer-directed philanthropic activity as an articulation of a quite disparate and messy set of forces that emanate both from within and outside of the state, the book is able to show how neoliberal thought is concretized in specific practices, and also how practices that are engaged in without particular political intention can end up reinforcing or, sometimes, threatening the neoliberal formation.[47] Building on the argument made by Jack Bratich, Jeremy Packer, and Cameron McCarthy in their introduction to *Foucault, Cultural Studies, and Governmentality,* then, the book seeks to show how breast cancer culture finds itself caught up in the processes of regulating conduct without a necessary reliance on the "codified, institutionalized" forms of governance.[48] The specific processes the book engages include discourses on individual responsibility and the character-building potential of volunteerism, the reconstitution of breast cancer as a "safe" disease, new marketing strategies designed to appeal to consumers' ethical sensibilities, and the creation of fund-raising tools that capitalize on the idea of physical exercise as a sign of healthy citizenship to produce active, rather than activist or armchair, philanthropists. Moreover, by highlighting the ways in which neoliberal governmentality is implicitly racialized and gendered, such that participation in consumer-oriented philanthropic activity represents a yardstick against which the capacities of individuals to become "proper" Americans are measured, it brings into question what can be rather universalizing accounts of neoliberal arts and rationalities of governing and the processes of subjectification that they enable.

Not surprisingly, the conjuncture of social forces that I have begun to map here go unacknowledged when proponents of philanthropic citizenship claim, as they repeatedly do, that it is a universal and inclusive category, external to the realm of politics, transcendent of economic concerns, and free of the socially divisive forces of race and gender. Nobody, they argue, can be opposed to ordinary folks doing good deeds for one another; philanthropic citizenship is something that we can all support and participate in regardless of our social location or political leanings. In contrast to this line of thought, and in keeping with the traditions of political engagement within cultural studies scholarship, *Pink Ribbons, Inc.* shows how such renderings rely on the erasure of power relations that undergird charitable works and seeks to confront the deeply class-structured, racialized, and gendered deployment of philanthropic practice as an ideal of citizenship.

Pink Ribbons, Inc.

Chapter 1, "A Dream Cause: Breast Cancer, Corporate Philanthropy, and the Market for Generosity," maps the transformation of corporate philanthropy over the past two decades from a relatively random, eclectic, and unscientific activity to a highly calculated and measured strategy that is integral to a business's profit-making function. Breast-cancer-related marketing has emerged as a highly prominent and successful example of this new approach, as products ranging from cars to yogurt have been sold to consumers with the promise that their purchase will help "raise awareness" of breast cancer or find a cure for the disease. In addition to highlighting the historical forces that helped produce cause-related marketing, the chapter examines the racialized and gendered norms and values that are circulated through breast cancer campaigns by businesses such as the National Football League.

The second chapter, "Doing Good by Running Well: The Race for the Cure and the Politics of Civic Fitness," explores the history and cultural significance of physical-activity-based fund-raising events, or "thons," and the particular dominance of breast-cancer-related events within this genre of charitable work. An ethnographic account of the Susan G. Komen Breast Cancer Foundation's Race for the Cure, now the largest network of 5K runs in the world, highlights the political identities and affiliations that are enabled and constrained by these forms of collective activity in a broader context in which consumerism has come to be recognized as a form of political action.

In chapter 3, "Stamping Out Breast Cancer: The Neoliberal State and the Volunteer Citizen," I reconstruct the history of the breast cancer research stamp. The creation of the stamp is analyzed within the context of the rise of neoliberalism as the dominant organizing principle of government and the economy in the United States since the 1970s and the renewed interest in philanthropy it has brought with it. In addition, by highlighting the particular versions of motherhood and femininity deployed in congressional and mass media discourse on the stamp, and in fund-raising for breast cancer more generally, it brings into question the widely held assumption that the popular appeal of breast cancer as a charitable cause reflects a radical transformation, for the better, in societal approaches to women's health.

Having successfully captured U.S. public interest in breast cancer, nonprofit organizations, pharmaceutical companies, and corporations have recently begun to pursue breast-cancer-related activities overseas. Describing itself as the "leading corporate supporter in the battle against breast cancer," the Avon corporation is responsible for running the most extensive "global" breast cancer program. The entry of businesses and nonprofit organizations into transnational philanthropic endeavors raises a number of important questions related to corporate giving, women's health, and global capitalism. In particular, chapter 4, "Imperial Charity: Women's Health, Cause-Related Marketing, and Global Capitalism," focuses on the social commitments that are enabled and constrained when "economic freedom" is pursued through the language and structures of global corporate philanthropy. It also questions how the use of breast cancer as the specific vehicle through which corporate interests are advanced might shape the social history of the disease on a "global" scale.

The fifth chapter of the book, "The Culture of Survivorship and the Tyranny of Cheerfulness," explores the materialization of the "breast cancer survivor" as a category of identity alongside the "tyranny of cheerfulness" that characterizes breast cancer culture in the United States at this time. The chapter opens with a discussion of the multifaceted challenge, in the 1970s, to the traditionally hierarchical relations that defined interactions between medical researchers, doctors, and patients and a general shift away from established notions of the "proper" medical patient as passive, unquestioning, and deferential. Drawing on the history of the AIDS movement, it suggests that the recognition that identity categories can significantly shape the course of a disease has had profound implications for the formation and strategies of the breast cancer movement. Through an analysis of the various forms of cultural work that have resulted in the gradual disappearance of the label "cancer victim," it traces how a notion of the empowered patient—the survivor—has become institutionalized and incorporated into the fabric of the cancer establishment. It also assesses the extent to which the market-driven, optimistic culture of survivorship is implicated in the exclusion of issues such as access to health care, poverty, and environmental racism from the agenda of the mainstream breast cancer movement and the political and medical institutions it is ostensibly seeking to change.

In the book's conclusion, "Beyond Pink Ribbons," I seek to highlight what is at stake in contemporary philanthropic practice as it relates to consumer culture. What are the most troubling characteristics of organized giving around breast cancer, and "American generosity" more broadly? And where can we see promise in these social relations as they are currently configured?

Chapter 1

✐ Dream Cause

Breast Cancer, Corporate Philanthropy, and the Market for Generosity

In the past, perhaps the wife of the CEO was particularly concerned about Alzheimer's so the company would donate money to that cause. The big sea change came when companies realized that this is actually corporate strategy. Now, the question about charity is, can it support corporate business?
—Carol Cone, *The New Republic*

In an oft-recited story, Nancy Brinker, founder of the Susan G. Komen Breast Cancer Foundation and Bush-appointed U.S. Ambassador to Hungary from 2001 to 2003, tells how she approached an executive of a lingerie manufacturer to suggest that they include a tag in their bras reminding customers to get regular mammograms. In response, the executive told Brinker, "We sell glamour. We don't sell fear. Breast cancer has nothing to do with our customers."[1] The fortunes of Brinker and the Komen Foundation have clearly changed since 1984, when this event is said to have taken place. Nancy Brinker is now recognized as a pioneer of cause-related marketing, and the Komen Foundation has more than a dozen national sponsors, a Million Dollar Council made up of twenty businesses that donate at least one million dollars per year, and a slew of other corporate partnerships at both local and national levels. They even have a contract with a lingerie company, Walcoal, to manufacture an "awareness bra."

While Brinker is recognized as a particularly adept procurer of corporate sponsorships, the Komen Foundation's partnerships are part of a larger trend that has seen upbeat and optimistic breast cancer campaigns become a central and integral part of the marketing strategy of numerous large corporations over the past ten years.[2] During this time, Avon, BMW, Bristol Myers Squibb, Estée Lauder, Ford Motor Company, General Electric,

General Motors, J. C. Penney, Kellogg's, Lee Jeans, and the National Football League have all turned to breast cancer philanthropy as a new and profitable strategy through which to market their products. Moreover, the nonprofit and advocacy groups with which they have aligned themselves are among the most high-profile players in the breast cancer movement.

Clearly the gradual destigmatization of breast cancer goes some way to explaining corporate interest in this particular cause; at the same time, this interest has aided in the process of destigmatization. In order to trace the historical conditions that have made the disease the "darling of corporate America," however, it is also necessary to consider broader shifts in the practice of corporate philanthropy and marketing over the past two decades.[3] During this time, a broad cultural preoccupation with philanthropic solutions to social problems, the discourse of efficiency and cost-cutting in business practice, changing psychological conceptions of the consumer, and invigorated consumer demands for a more ethical form of capitalism have converged to produce the transformation of corporate philanthropy from a relatively random, eclectic, and unscientific activity to a highly calculated and measured strategy that is integral to a business's profit-making function.

The contention here is not that tools such as breast-cancer-related marketing, which have emerged as part of this general shift, are simply manipulation or propaganda that imposes meanings and values on docile consumers or incites false desires in the name of "diffusing or neutralizing political unrest."[4] Rather, it is that these are techniques by which to understand, represent, and act upon the desires of consumers to be generous and civic-minded citizens in the service of selling products. The effect, I shall argue, is a new form of subsidized philanthropy (in cause-related marketing campaigns, corporations might best be understood as vectors for the transfer of money spent by consumers on designated products to the nonprofits in whose name the products are sold) and often advertising (resources, other than money, donated as a result of cause marketing campaigns are tax deductible). In addition, these tools produce a constant flow of images suggesting that the key to solving America's problems lies in corporate philanthropy, personal generosity, and proper consumption. While cause-related marketing sells goods through this promise, it also packages generosity as a lifestyle choice through which individuals can attain self-actualization and self-realization by, for example, subscribing to a Working Assets long-distance plan so that for each phone call a percentage of the charge will be donated to a nonprofit organization.

Such symbolic effects are the focus of the second part of the chapter, a case study of a National Football League breast cancer marketing campaign. Through an analysis of the articulation of popular anxieties about crime and character in the NFL to discourses on player volunteerism, it explores how the class-inflected, racially coded, and gender normative ethos of generosity offered up for consumption through this campaign is suggestive of the political stakes and dangers bound up with cause-related marketing as a mode of governing desire.

Corporate Philanthropy: A Historical Perspective

It was the New Jersey Supreme Court in 1953 that ruled on the legality of corporate donations. Two years previously, the board of directors of A. P. Smith Manufacturing had donated $1,500 to Princeton University for general maintenance purposes. Several stockholders challenged the legitimacy of the gift in the New Jersey courts by charging that this was a misappropriation of corporate funds and went beyond corporate powers because the company's charter did not explicitly authorize such donations. The judge, however, ruled in favor of the company, whose president had argued that he considered his contribution to be sound because the public expects such philanthropy from corporations, because it would obtain goodwill for the company in the community, and because it would further the company's self-interest in assuring a continual flow of well-trained personnel for employment in the corporate world.[5] Significantly, the court also argued that with the transfer of wealth from individuals to corporations and with the "burdens of taxation resulting from increased state and federal aid," corporations were expected to assume the modern obligations of good citizenship just as individuals had in the past. Such giving was also necessary, the court argued, to ensure the survival of private educational institutions and thus of the "system of free enterprise." In subsequent legal challenges, state courts ruled that corporations were free to give to charities whether or not they were related to the business of the company. These rulings opened the door for corporate support of local and national charities, and corporate funding in support of the arts and education, in particular, increased dramatically.[6]

Although the development of government social welfare programs under the New Deal marked a turn toward social democracy, the development of the idea of an "associative state" was crucial to the institutionalization and expansion of corporate philanthropy in the years following World War II. Business leaders such as Frank Abrams of Standard Oil of New Jersey, Alfred P. Sloan of General Motors, and Arthur W. Page of AT&T created the Council for Aid to Education to encourage corporate support for higher education because they believed that by funding private universities, businesses might stem the growth of government-supported public education and the expansion of government programs more generally that had resulted from the war, the New Deal, and particularly the enactment of the GI Bill.[7] As a result, the belief in philanthropy as a vehicle for preventing or stemming the growth of a welfare state remained an enduring justification for corporate philanthropy through the course of the twentieth century.

While these business leaders maintained an ambitious vision for the role of philanthropy, from the 1950s to the 1980s corporate giving moved away from its position at the center of business activity to assume a more peripheral and independent role.[8] Although philanthropy was viewed as valuable insofar as it enhanced a corporation's reputation, it was not yet viewed as a tool that could be employed directly in the service of selling goods.[9] This was to change, however, in the last two decades of the twentieth century—a period in which the philosophy and practice of corporate philanthropy underwent rapid transformation. While there are instances in which corporations make financial contributions without reference to their markets or overall strategic plans, most large corporations now employ a business-driven approach to contributions as they seek to attach "value," "strategic vision," and "mission" to their charitable activities. This business-driven approach is known as "strategic philanthropy" and requires that every dollar given must mesh with the company's markets or employees and work as part of their overall strategic plans.

Reaganomics and the Rise of Strategic Philanthropy

It was during the tenure of the Reagan administration, according to Elizabeth Boris (director of the Center on Nonprofits and Philanthropy), that "nonprofit organizations were propelled to U.S. public consciousness."[10] In 1981, Reagan had created the Task Force on Private Sector Initiatives to encourage private sector activity in social programs and increase nongovernmental sources of support for nonprofits. "Volunteerism," Reagan declared, "is an essential part of our plan to give government back to the people. I believe the people are anxious for this responsibility. . . . We can show the world how to construct a social system more humane, more compassionate, and more effective in meeting its members' needs than any ever known."[11] Concurrently, the administration introduced incentives by reducing corporate taxes and increasing the limits on charitable deductions for corporations from 5 to 10 percent of taxable income.[12]

At the same time that the nonprofit sector was called upon to partner with corporations to develop private sector alternatives to public welfare (which was said to stifle the volunteer impulses of private citizens and private business), the nonprofit sector saw its budget reduced significantly and its client rolls increase as a result of the administration's cuts in welfare spending and an ongoing recession.[13] These cuts, combined with the considerable public attention focused on private sector initiatives prompted by the launching of the Task Force, coincided to produce a substantial increase in the number of requests on the part of nonprofits for aid from corporations.

Over 75 percent of the executives surveyed for a 1981 Conference Board report said that requests for aid from nonprofits had jumped substantially, with some reporting a 300 percent increase.[14] Although these changes appear to have had an impact on corporate giving in the short term (that is, until 1987 and the onset of the recession), there was no significant increase in contributions favoring human services. In other words, the increased level of corporate contributions facilitated by Reagan's tax cuts and incentives (which anyway fell far short of the estimated $29 million needed to "bridge the gap") did not flow to those areas of provision—economic development, hunger relief, or job training, for instance—most affected by cuts in expenditure.[15]

Large corporations such as AT&T and leading business organizations such as the Business Roundtable linked their support for the Reagan tax and spending cuts to increases in corporate philanthropy.[16] If business was serious "in seeking to stem over-dependence on government," the Roundtable contended, it had to "increase its level of commitment" to the nonprofit sector.[17] However, when the cuts were actually instituted, business leaders did not express enthusiasm or intent to fill the gap set out by administration strategists. According to Sophia Muirhead, executives claimed that although their contributions had tripled between 1976 and 1985 from $1.5 billion to $4.5 billion, the $29 billion gap left by Reagan's cuts was too large for corporations to realistically close. Positioning business as an isolated socioeconomic entity that had been called upon by the state to respond to a problem in which businesses themselves were not seen to be implicated, corporate leaders were said to "resent the transfer of the social burden and responsibility to the private sector."[18] In this vein, one unnamed corporate executive told the Conference Board, "We didn't start these programs . . . and we shouldn't be responsible for their continuation if federal money is not available." And an unnamed "Public Affairs Vice President" said, "Our company supported [President Reagan] because we believed in the elimination of a number of these programs. Naturally, we're not too enthused about continuing the programs and shifting the burden to the corporate sector."[19]

The Reagan administration's cuts in Social Security spending coincided with rising unemployment brought about by deindustrialization and a spate of deregulation-induced corporate mergers, diversification, restructuring, and downsizing that had begun in the late 1970s. As businesses merged, downsized, and streamlined, corporate contributions became the focus of managers who were seeking to gain efficiency in an increasingly competitive marketplace. In the words of James P. Shannon, a corporate philanthropy consultant and recognized proponent of the shift to strategic philanthropy, these changes "put the current managers of corporate philanthropy on notice that henceforth their departments would be evaluated by management against the same standards of performance, efficiency, production, and achievement as all other departments in their companies."[20] As a result, some contributions programs disappeared, while others were streamlined. Barry Lastra, a public affairs consultant with the Chevron Corporation, describes the impact of the Chevron-Gulf merger on their corporate giving function as follows:

> In melding corporate contributions, one plus one seldom equals two. When Gulf's $10.2 million contributions budget was combined with Chevron's $20 million contributions budget there was an immediate 11 percent reduction to a combined program of $27 million. . . . A merger forces an overall analytical review that is invaluable—my experience would suggest this type of critical review is in order even without the trauma of a corporate merger.[21]

Lastra also articulates here the widespread belief in the need to streamline corporate contributions *in general,* even in times of relative economic stability—a belief that has been widely put into practice since the early 1990s.

As pressure increased for efficiency and restraint in corporate contributions, a key shift occurred. Staff in these areas began to look for ways to make philanthropic activities profitable, and strategic philanthropy emerged as the solution. Thus, when Kodak's community relations and contributions program faced a decrease in its budget, its staff strove to make "community relations a strategic resource in gaining revenue for the company." Kodak's new strategy involved partnerships between the contributions department and other units of the business so that these units would learn "the value of investing in urban markets," "promote business-to-business relationships—not just philanthropic ones—with nonprofits," "leverage contributions to enhance sales opportunities," and "make grants that enhance global access."[22] Thus, Kodak's philanthropic and profit-making functions became inextricably intertwined, as philanthropy is viewed as a possible route to gaining access to new markets at home and abroad, finding new partners with whom to do business, and enhancing sales.

Kodak's shift toward strategic philanthropy is typical of corporate America's move to "treat donations like investments" and thus to "expect some return from them," a move that simultaneously represents a turn away from the understanding of philanthropy as a more straightforward obligation of corporate citizenship.[23] By the 1990s, management guru Peter Drucker's argument that altruism cannot be the criterion by which corporate giving is evaluated had become a guiding assumption of contributions programs as businesses discharged their social responsibilities by converting them into self-interest and hence business opportunities.[24]

As executives have searched for ways to make corporate philanthropy profitable, they have also sought ways to make it more scientific. Referring to the effect of demands for efficiency on corporate contributions departments, James P. Shannon wrote, "The problem posed by these new standards is that until now many corporate giving programs have had no clear mission statement, no regular documentation of their effectiveness and no systematic way of measuring whether or how their work products complement the mission or the strategic plans of their parent companies."[25] Similarly, Craig Smith, president of Corporate Citizen (a corporate philanthropy consulting firm) and another leader in the move toward strategic philanthropy, called for increased research in the field and argued that "if corporate philanthropy is to flourish or even survive, it will be at least in part because researchers have generated the theoretic framework, the methodologies, measurements, and data that show skeptical corporate executives how corporate philanthropy assists corporate competitive strategies."[26]

From these developments, a new generation of philanthropic consultants trained in the principles of business administration has emerged. The role of these consultants is to develop appropriate strategies and research methods to decide how and where to distribute grants and other resources and to help corporations develop systems for tracking the effectiveness of their giving programs in terms of both impact on their designated social problems and profitability. Thus, instead of merely giving in reaction to appeals for charitable grants, the process has become proactive, with budgetary priorities, program planning, coordination, and accountability. In turn, it is these professionals who have been charged with inventing a vast array of tools, plans, strategies, and techniques for governing philanthropic activities.[27]

In practice, the shift toward strategic philanthropy has meant that most large corporations have undertaken at least some of the following changes in their approach to philanthropy and community relations: the use of a narrow focus or theme, such as environmental protection, breast cancer, or youth literacy, to maximize the impact of giving and to align contributions with the company's business goals and brand characteristics; the support of programs that target beneficiaries who are or could become customers; the integration of the company's giving program with other departments such as marketing, public affairs, and government relations; the formation of partnerships with community groups, local governments, and other companies that share a common interest in a particular concern; the development of volunteer programs with awards, matching gifts, paid-volunteer time, or other incentives to encourage employees to serve their communities; the instigation of global volunteering or grant-making programs that emphasize and attain a "worldwide" presence; the utilization of already existing company resources to enable noncash forms of contributions; the use of public relations campaigns that highlight company activities; and an increased emphasis on the measurement of program results.[28]

The development of these tools and tactics of strategic philanthropy point to the extent to which a practice that was previously relatively random, eclectic, unscientific, and based largely on the individual preferences of high-ranking corporate leaders has been transformed into a highly calculated, measured, quantified, and planned approach to giving or "charitable investing." The effect of this transformation has been to place philanthropy at the center of business activity and to transform it into a revenue-producing mechanism. This has occurred at exactly the moment in which activist demands for a more responsible corporate citizenship have gained considerable strength and public attention and has allowed corporations to point to their strategic philanthropy initiatives as evidence of their heightened responsibility and compassion.

Cause-Related Marketing

Of all the tools of strategic philanthropy that have emerged since the early 1990s, cause-related marketing is one of the most widely used and publicly visible, in part because it is understood to accomplish efficiently the integration of a corporation's philanthropic activities with its drive for profit. Cause-related marketing emerged in the mid-1980s as a strategic marketing tool for differentiating a brand and adding value to it. Carol Cone, founder and CEO of Cone Communications, a firm that earns more than $4 million per year promoting cause-related marketing, explains the turn to this new strategy as follows: "No one wants to compete on the basis of price or innovation. Everyone can cut prices, and with today's technology any innovation can be copied within ninety days."[29] Instead, companies and brands associate themselves with a cause as a means to build the reputation of a brand, increase profit, develop employee loyalty to the company, and add to their reputation as good corporate citizens.[30]

Unlike traditional charity promotions in which a brand or company simply donated money to a cause or sponsored a range of unrelated charities without a coherent strategy, cause-related marketing seeks to ensure that the brand and the cause share the same "territory" in a "living, altruistic partnership for mutual benefit." Thus, since the mid-1990s, cause-related marketing has evolved from what were mostly short-term commitments from corporations to their chosen causes—that is, a one- or two-month promotion with a charitable organization at the end of which the corporation donated a portion of its profits—to major, long-term commitments to an issue through an alliance that links the company or brand name with the issue in the consumer's mind. According to marketing professionals, the short-term approach is gradually giving way to the long-term approach as the former has come to be seen as opportunistic and therefore possibly harmful to a company's image. Moreover, weak links between a cause and a company are thought to increase the likelihood that a corporation appears to be "cashing in" on other people's misfortune. From the marketer's perspective, longer-term programs have a measure of built-in immunity to charges of opportunism. In addition, short-term promotions are not thought to shore up the association between the brand and the cause for consumers, and thus fail to "build the brand" in the desired manner.[31]

Marketing experts frequently refer to cause-related marketing as a means to "cut through the clutter" caused by increasing competition between manufacturers, the power of multiple retailers, technological advances, fragmentation of media audiences, and the increase in the sheer volume of commercial communications directed at the market. Hence, cause-related marketing is understood as a "filter," a way to attract the attention and loyalty of the consumer, who is understood to be increasingly adept at reading marketing messages and dissecting the meaning and symbolism of any particular commercial or advertisement.[32]

In so-called developing markets, experts claim, the priority for marketers and brands is to achieve rapid gains in consumer "penetration" and market share: "The battle is all about acquiring new customers before the competition does."[33] However, in more "mature" markets like the United States, where growth is slow and steady, if it exists at all, marketers have decided that new customer acquisition strategies are expensive and that the pursuit of brand share (that is the struggle to make their brand the dominant brand in consumers' imaginations) often comes at the expense of profitability. In these markets, practitioners increasingly focus their attention on retaining customers and building loyalty to their brands.

Marketing professionals are explicit in their belief that cause-related marketing should be first and foremost a strategy for selling products, rather than an altruistic or philanthropic activity. For instance, public relations consultant Jennifer Mullen, writing in *Public Relations Quarterly,* points out that cause marketing has emerged as "corporations increasingly want added value for their charitable giving activities."[34] Writing in the *Harvard Business Review,* Jerry Welsh, the president of Welsh Marketing Associates, expresses his concern that some cause-related marketing campaigns do not give consumers a good reason to remember the company or brand "at the end of the day":

> Cause related marketing was meant to be marketing, not philanthropy. Otherwise we would know it as "marketing related philanthropy" or something to that effect. The practice was aptly named, however, to describe an innovative and socially useful way to augment the power of more traditional marketing, promotion, and public relations efforts.[35]

Mullen even goes so far as to suggest that cause-related marketing campaigns might help save a company's reputation at a time when it is brought into disrepute:

> Consumers who believe a corporation is ethical may be more likely to have preconceived notions and positive expectations, and they may give the benefit of the doubt in otherwise difficult situations such as negative publicity stemming from a crisis.[36]

Moreover, a recent report of the Conference Board suggested that the very idea of corporate philanthropy might be questionable in the light of the rise of cause-related marketing and other aspects of strategic philanthropy:

> The appropriateness of the term "philanthropy" to describe corporate giving is being debated. As companies are increasingly driven to analyze the return they're getting for their donations, the process is becoming one of *financially sound goodwill*. (Emphasis added)[37]

Marketers and the corporations for whom they work overwhelmingly view cause-related marketing as a successful business strategy. According to oft-quoted statistics from Mintel Marketing Intelligence, American Express's campaign in the late 1980s to raise funds for the renovation of the Statue of Liberty generated an estimated $1.7 million for the cause, a 27 percent increase in card usage, and a 10 percent jump in new card membership applications.[38] Condé Nast reader surveys on the Ford Community Action Team breast cancer campaign found that 63 percent of readers said it "made them feel better about Ford Motor" and that the number of women who would consider purchasing a Ford product the next time they are in the market is increasing.[39]

While marketing professionals are usually explicit about the profit motive behind such marketing, they often explain the emergence of cause-related marketing as a reflection of a shift in consumer attitudes. In this vein, Bill Laberis, editor of *Computerworld* magazine, said of contemporary American consumers, "They want something to believe in, whether it's family, a set of values or some passion they can pursue. . . . [It's a] kind of spirituality." Robert Eckert, then president and CEO of Kraft Foods, told the annual meeting of the Association of National Advertisers, "Consumers are yearning to connect to people and things that will give meaning to their lives."[40]

We can glean from these examples that marketing discourse, like the popular media, understood and represented the 1990s—in contrast to the alleged self-centeredness and greed of the previous decade—as a more ethical era in American history, a decade of "values," "decency," "spirituality," and "generosity." Whereas in the 1980s, "brands successfully constructed ravishing imagery, enlisted psychological tricks and built aspirational style on TV," in the "'morning after' decade of the 90s, the consumer pendulum has swung back to a concern with intrinsic values and the market is less convinced by cosmetic displays."[41] Thus, Hamish Pringle and Marjorie Thompson claim, "There is growing evidence that consumers are looking for new sorts of brand values. These go well beyond the practical issues of functional product performance or rational product benefits and further than the emotional and psychological aspects of brand personality and image." "Consumers," they claim, are "moving towards the top of Maslow's hierarchy of needs and seeking self-realization." In other words, "material wealth is decreasingly relevant to personal happiness as the desire for 'belonging,' 'self-esteem' and 'self-realization' become more important."[42] Such claims are frequently accompanied by reference to market research by companies such as Cone Communications that suggests that consumers are more likely to select a brand if it is associated with a cause they care about.[43] Thus, while cause-related marketing is, on the one hand, a response to consumer desires as these desires are constituted through technologies of market research, it is, on the other hand, a tool for *incorporating* heightened consumer interest in corporate ethics as "people are asking more and more questions about the role of commercial organizations in society and are looking for demonstrations of good corporate citizenship."[44]

In this respect, marketing discourse on the desire of the consumer to find meaning in life through ethical consumption converges with social science discourse on declining civic trust:

> There has been an alarming decline in the levels of trust in the traditional institutions, the pillars of community such as the Church, government, and the police to which people had been accustomed to "belonging" or from which many had gained their sense of social direction and moral authority.[45]

Pringle and Thompson's words sound remarkably similar to those of writers such as political scientist Robert Putnam, who argued in a widely circulated and debated essay, "Bowling Alone," that Americans are less likely to join groups, volunteer, and participate than they have in the past and that this trend is an index of weakened "civil society" and a less healthy democracy.[46] Indeed, Pringle and Thompson suggest that as a mechanism with the potential to fulfill widespread desire for social direction and moral authority, cause-related marketing represents one possible solution to declining civic trust:

> While traditionalists may regret the demise of the previous pillars of society, the exciting prospect for the corporate beneficiaries of the situation is the possibility to leverage their well-earned degrees of consumer trust and confidence to their commercial benefit. This can be done through the technique of Cause Related Marketing. . . . If the sense of "belonging" which is so important to consumers, according to Maslow's theory, becomes reality, and there's not much left around to belong to in terms of traditional institutions, then perhaps newer ones, even brands, can step into the breech.[47]

Based on a survey of British voters, they even suggest that corporate sponsorship of elections might help increase voter turnout:

> Often obscure and perhaps even potentially intimidating routes to rarely visited village halls and community centers were a strong disincentive to many. By contrast, the possibility of casting a vote at the checkout of a local Safeway was very much more attractive and seen as bringing voting into the mainstream of daily life.[48]

Thus, the "threat" of global competition coexists with the "opportunities" presented by the "citizen's sense of alienation and lack of fulfillment," and cause-related marketing, they suggest, presents the most promising solution to this bind.[49]

While the development of cause marketing technologies represents an attempt to ascertain and measure "emerging customer demands for 'higher order attributes,'" that is, to find ways to satisfy consumer aspirations to be engaged and generous citizens, such technologies simultaneously constitute marketers as arbiters of ethical citizenship and civic virtue. "Belief systems must become part and parcel of the 'marketer's armory,'" Pringle and Thompson argue. Marketers, in other words, must extend their understanding and interpretation of a brand's "territory" "beyond the functional performance and emotional or aspirational imagery into that of 'ethics' and 'beliefs.'"[50]

What "ethics" and "beliefs" does cause-related marketing deploy? What forms of "social direction" and "moral authority" does it offer? What kinds of life and forms of conduct does it support? As the largest private funder of breast cancer research in the United States, one of the breast cancer movement's most prominent voices, and one of the pioneers of cause marketing in the United States, the Susan G. Komen Breast Cancer Foundation provides a potent site through which to explore these questions.

"Brand Aid, Cause Effective":
The Rise of Breast-Cancer-Related Marketing

Throughout the year, an array of large, well-known corporations stage special events to raise money for the Komen Foundation: BMW organizes the Ultimate Drive, a series of sponsored test-drives; *Golf for Women* magazine sponsors Rally for the Cure, in which women pay to play in golf tournaments at country clubs across the United States; Jazzercize stages the Art & Soul Tour in which participants pay a minimum of $150 for an afternoon of high-energy workouts; and KitchenAid, in conjunction with *Gourmet* magazine, encourages consumers to host Cook for the Cure fund-raising dinner parties. Other corporations, including Better Homes and Gardens, Boston Market, Dirt Devil, J. C. Penney, and Pier 1, hold promotions in which they donate a percentage of the sale price of "breast cancer awareness products" to the Komen Foundation.

During National Breast Cancer Awareness Month, in October, corporate activity to raise money for the Komen Foundation intensifies. In 2005, for example, Lee Jeans staged its tenth annual Lee National Denim Day, for which it asks corporations and businesses to allow their employees to wear denim to work on a chosen Friday in exchange for a five-dollar donation; American Airlines held its annual Celebrity Golf Weekend; Hallmark Gold Crown stores gave money raised from the sale of designated cards; the Republic of Tea ran its Sip for the Cure program, in which five pink fund-raising teas were offered to consumers; as part of its Caring for Both Ends of the Leash program, Breeder's Choice Pet Foods gave a donation for each bag of specially selected dog and cat food; and Yoplait placed breast cancer awareness messages on the lids of its yogurts with the promise that for every lid mailed in by consumers, they would donate ten cents to the Komen Foundation.[51]

As the opportunity to participate in raising money for breast cancer research has been used to sell products ranging from Hallmark cards to automobiles, breast cancer marketing has become the focus of much commentary and analysis among marketing experts seeking to understand and chart the passions, interests, and desires of contemporary consumers. Under headlines such as "Cancer Sells," these experts have labeled breast cancer "a dream cause" and pointed to the success of corporate campaigns against the disease as a way to encourage other companies to pursue cause-related marketing.[52]

There is, of course, an irony at work here. For, as numerous corporations have turned to breast cancer as a way to *differentiate* their products and to cut through the clutter of commercial communications, they have had the effect of making breast cancer marketing ubiquitous. In turn, this has produced intense competition as corporations struggle, in the words of Avon's Joanne Mazurki, "to gain ownership over the issue."[53] While this struggle has occasionally been enacted explicitly and with recourse to the law (when the Komen Foundation, for example, sought unsuccessfully to secure the breast cancer ribbon as its exclusive property or when they attempted, this time with success, to trademark the phrase "for the cure"), it has for the most part been evidenced in the diversification and expansion of breast cancer marketing.[54] That is, in the struggle to gain ownership over the ethos of generosity, corporations have invented new ways to differentiate their versions of generosity from those of their competitors.

Real Men Wear Pink: Breast Cancer and the NFL

In April 1999, the National Football League signed on as a national sponsor of the Susan G. Komen Breast Cancer Foundation's Race for the Cure.[55] This arrangement—which partnered a professional sports league that is the epitome of a racialized black hypermasculinity with a nonprofit that is the epitome of a pink-ribbon, racialized, white hyperfemininity—brought with it an immediate guarantee of product differentiation and recognition. Moreover, the announcement of the new partnership coincided with an ongoing effort on the part of the league to show, in the words of *Detroit News* writer Becky Yerak, "that it's in touch with its feminine side." Yerak continues: "New advertising and marketing campaigns by the National Football League . . . have begun muting the usual machismo and shaping pitches more to women, children and even men who aren't necessarily hard-core fans of the weekend showcase or alpha males." This new approach to marketing was created, in part, in response to a survey that found that 40 percent of the NFL's 113 million weekly television viewers are women and, of those 45 million, "20 million call themselves avid fans."[56] Hoping to maintain this market and to capture the interest of new fans, the NFL turned to breast cancer, an already tried and tested focus, for a cause marketing campaign.

In a press release announcing the deal, Nancy Brinker of the Komen Foundation and Sara Levinson of the NFL described their new partnership as an opportunity to spread the message of early detection to the league's huge fan base, which includes more than 68 million women.[57] Situating the promotion of mammography at the center of the campaign and pointing to the promise of this new alliance against cancer, Brinker said of the deal:

> We are thrilled to have an organization like the NFL as a national sponsor of Race for the Cure. This partnership will allow us to spread the life-saving message of early detection to millions of professional football fans, both women and men. With the support of NFL teams, players and fans, we can win the race against breast cancer.[58]

The sponsorship deal included a promise by the NFL to enhance marketing and "grassroots" support of the Komen Race for the Cure series. Grassroots activities were to include appearances by players and their families at race events, national television advertising, breast cancer detection information affixed to all "NFL for Her" merchandise, and race sign-ups at NFL Workshops for Women.[59]

DeAnn Forbes, owner of a "female-owned" advertising agency that has a contract with the Detroit Lions to stimulate women's interest in the game, explained the NFL's new approach as follows:

> People are tired of seeing a guy in a uniform and another guy in a uniform. Human interest is what'll bring a broader audience. . . . Whether it's the average fan or novice, they want to know what drives these players. The only way you can really feel connected is to see them, hear them, know them.[60]

Thus, the NFL's campaign was designed to stimulate what is understood as the (albeit unstated) peculiarly female desire for human interest and personal interaction. And as this discourse helped constitute women, in contrast to men, as more emotional and more in need of such interaction, it also helped solidify historically embedded links between women, nurturing, and benevolence.

Beginning in October 1999, to coincide with Breast Cancer Awareness Month, the NFL aired a selection of six different TV spots featuring NFL players to "help raise awareness and encourage fans to join in the fight against breast cancer."[61] The spots, titled "Real Mean Wear Pink," aired during NFL games and prime-time and daytime programming on ABC, CBS, ESPN, and FOX. Each spot was tagged with a logo bearing the NFL shield wrapped around a pink ribbon and a phone number that provided information about Race for the Cure events. The footage for the spots was filmed in July 1999 at the Race for the Cure in Aspen, Colorado, a week before the opening of NFL training camps. Press releases created to accompany the airing of the spots emphasized the details of the players' involvement. To ensure the authenticity of the players' commitment, the release explained that they did their "unscripted" voice-overs during a group discussion before and after the event.[62]

Each of the commercials was visually similar: hundreds of white, middle-aged women (along with smaller numbers of white men and children), decked out in pink and white athletic apparel, walking and jogging along the tree-lined streets of Aspen. Interspersed with these images was footage of the featured players (four of whom are the only people of color visible in the commercials), erecting banners and signs, handing out water to participants as they run by, shaking hands with the men, holding hands with the children, and hugging the women.

In each commercial, the featured players described their appreciation and admiration for the courage and pride of the survivors: "There's nothing like the look of the survivor," Jamal Anderson said, "and you look into their eyes and you can't help but be overwhelmed." Similarly, Tony Gonzalez declared, "Man, these people are the true warriors. Man, they're out there struggling with life and death. It's just . . . it's an inspiration for me." Hardy Nickerson explained:

> Once I got to the race and started talking to people and started hearing their stories, I think that was the most uplifting part about the whole Race for the Cure. Once you get around the survivors, man, they tell you "I've been a survivor for thirty years." "I've been a survivor for forty years." I found myself caught up and just wanting to talk to everybody and wanting to hear all the stories.

These voice-overs were accompanied by long, lingering close-up shots of the faces of individual survivors (identified by their pink visors and T-shirts). As the players expressed their admiration for breast cancer survivors, they also described how their experiences at the race had inspired them to "do more" for the cause. Gonzalez said it was something he might "wanna do in the future," while Anderson suggested that their participation "might help make next year's race bigger" and that it "hopefully raised the awareness of what the Komen Foundation was trying to do." Nickerson pointed to the uplifting stories of survivorship as a motivation to bring more people into the fight against breast cancer: "The more you hear the stories the more encouraged you get and the more encouraged you get, the more you're able to encourage someone else. That's what life is all about." Kordell Stewart, who described his mother's battle with breast cancer and her living ten years after diagnosis instead of the one year predicted by doctors, says: "It's about these people out here who are struggling with cancer and not knowing if they're gonna make it or not. But yet, if we come out here and just give a helping hand they might get an extra year or so. You just don't know how strong the mind is."

Real Men Have Character: Crime and Punishment in the NFL

In tone and style—the sentimental, personal narratives, the soft focus shots, the pink-and-white color scheme, the uplifting music—the NFL campaign was in many ways a typical breast-cancer-related marketing effort. While the significance of the campaign lay partly in its capacity for attracting new consumers, however, we cannot reduce its significance, or that of cause-related marketing in general, to the production of new markets. Nor can we begin to understand its implications simply by undertaking a close textual reading of the commercials. Indeed, what makes it a particularly interesting site for analysis is that it condensed a range of issues related to the gender and racial politics of philanthropy. In order to highlight these issues and to read to the campaign contextually, it is useful to take a brief detour through debates about what has come to be known as the "character issue" in the NFL—that is, the alleged propensity of NFL players to criminality, and concomitant debates among officials, coaches, and media critics about how best to screen out "undesirable characters" when recruiting new players to join the league.

Public discussions about the world of professional basketball and football have long been a site for the expression of cultural anxieties about race, crime, and violence. Cheryl Cole argues that during the 1980s, popular knowledge about the inner city, urban problems, and black masculinity was produced and rendered visible through the categories of "sport" and "gangs," where sport appeared as the locus of "conventional values" such as a healthy lifestyle, productivity, and discipline, and gangs as the site for those behaviors that were thought to threaten such values—out-of-control violence, insatiable consumerism, and a refusal to take proper and meaningful employment.[63] In turn, such behaviors were deemed responsible for the devastation and "disorder" of America's inner cities. The sport-gang dyad, while ensuring that the values articulated to both sport and gangs remain unquestioned, does not guarantee black athletes an escape from the discourse of racism. For the sport-gang dyad also works as a normalizing lens *within* the world of sport: the criminalization and pathologization of black masculinity is so deeply inscribed and so utterly pervasive as to make African American athletes, like all African American men, always potential criminals. Hence, the mass media presents the American public with a constant flow of stories detailing the lives of professional athletes who have apparently been unable to abandon the modes of conduct allegedly instilled in them from a young age. Sports researcher Jeff Benedict makes this point explicit when he claims in an interview with *Sport* that "you can take the boy out of the inner city but you can't take the inner city out of the boy."[64]

Although the alleged propensity of athletes to criminal behavior has been well established in the popular imagination for some while, a proliferation of discourse on the "character issue" surfaced around the time of the release of the Race for the Cure commercials.[65] When Lawrence Phillips, a player known for his "past bad behavior," was drafted by the St. Louis Rams in 1996 and subsequently arrested on a number of occasions for a variety of offenses, all the subject of intense media coverage, NFL team owners introduced a violent-crime policy by which players arrested for such crimes would be subject to therapy, fines, suspension, or banishment depending on the type of crime committed and the verdict reached by the courts.[66] The Phillips affair was followed, in 1998, by the publication of Jeff Benedict and Don Yaeger's *Pros and Cons: The Criminals Who Play in the NFL,* "the most highly anticipated sports book of the year," according to sportswriter Armen Keteyian. Benedict and Yaeger's "explosive exposé" purported to reveal the "shocking percentage" of NFL players who have been formally charged with committing a serious crime such as rape, domestic violence, assault, battery, and DUI.[67] Responding to charges by NFL officials that the book would "unfavorably serve to perpetuate stereotypes" and "may, in fact, have been racist," coauthor Benedict told *Sport* magazine that the fact that "so many athletic offenders are black is not a function of race, but rather of the rising recruitment of poorly prepared young men, the majority of whom are black, whose social backgrounds are rife with problems."[68]

The NFL's response to the book was to commission its own survey of crime in the League. And when the debate over crime, character, and the NFL reached new heights in the early months of 2000 with the arrest of two high profile players (Rae Carruth of the Carolina Panthers and Ray Lewis of the Baltimore Ravens) on charges of murder within the space of a few weeks, NFL Commissioner Paul Tagliabue had the survey findings on hand.[69] Professional football players, Tagliabue declared, committed crimes at a rate commensurate with the general population "of the same age and racial background."[70] Thus, as the NFL attempted to undermine the notion that athletes are somehow predisposed to criminal behavior, their response only served to confirm this notion.

Under headlines such as "NFL: National Felons League," the media set about trying to explain this "unfathomable" set of circumstances and to seek solutions to the "character issue."[71] The theories proffered as explanations ranged from the violent nature of the sport, to the dangers and temptations of women (the "evil that lurks in skirts" according to Diane Shah of the *Chicago Sun-Times*), to the background or "environment" from which the players originate, to their upbringing in female-headed, "welfare" families.[72] The solutions put forward by the NFL and legitimized in media discourse on the situation included more intense education for rookies, therapy for violence-prone players, more thorough character screening during the drafting process (NFL teams already perform extensive background checks and psychological testing on potential recruits), and a greater emphasis on character-building practices such as volunteerism.

The NFL has also proposed dealing with the character issue by emphasizing, through mass media campaigns, "the positive deeds players do in the community" and encouraging "wives and girlfriends to participate more in the programs designed to help players stay out of trouble."[73] Thus, in line with the recommendations of cause-related marketing experts such as Jennifer Mullen, who, as we saw previously, suggests that such campaigns may give corporations the "benefit of the doubt" during moments of negative publicity, the NFL views marketing tools such as Real Men Wear Pink as vehicles for repairing their public image. Moreover, the league looks to women, who are thus reaffirmed as the moral guardians of men, as key to the ethical transformation of their "troubled" players.

The importance of professional athletes' participation in philanthropy or volunteerism is understood, moreover, to go beyond its public relations potential. As the media scrutinized Lewis's "character," for instance, they also looked to his record of philanthropic or volunteer activities to strengthen their assessments. In an extended analysis of the Lewis case, Jarret Bell asks if we should understand Lewis as a "saint or thug." One interviewee, Ronald Cherry, a Baltimore lawyer who had "known Lewis for four years," told Bell that "Lewis is easily one of the nicest men I've ever met."[74] For evidence to support Cherry's claim, Bell turns to Lewis's "involvement in the community as a testament to his character":

> Lewis is considered a "go-to" guy by the Ravens' staff because of his generosity with time and money for needy causes. He routinely visits children in hospitals, and he became active with the Police Athletic League in Baltimore. He once purchased 250 tickets for underprivileged kids to attend a Washington Bullets (now Wizards) game, and he hosted a bowling tournament to aid needy kids. And Lewis once matched the team's $23,000 contribution to a food drive.

"But," Bell continues, making explicit the apparent disjuncture between a propensity toward volunteering and a propensity toward crime, "Lewis has also been the focus of police interest."[75]

Following Lewis's and Carruth's respective arrests, the NFL draft became the focus for further discussion of the character issue. In the run-up to the draft, league general managers "talked endlessly about picking players with character,"[76] and when the New York Jets drafted "three players with rap sheets,"[77] critics expressed their skepticism.[78] Alongside details of these players' "troubled ways," critics drew attention to new draftees who scored highly on character tests and articulated their scores to their realizing the importance of volunteerism: LaVar Arrington, who was drafted by the Redskins, "spoke about responsibility and character," and Chris Samuels, also picked by the Redskins, "visited with inner city kids in Brooklyn during his stay in New York." Unlike officials at the New York Jets, Arrington and Samuels "get it," claimed Gary Myers of the *New York Daily News.* And what do they get? we might ask. That "character counts."[79]

Building "Proper" Citizens: The Pedagogy of Volunteerism and the Racialization of Generosity

How then should we read the Real Men Wear Pink campaign? What does this campaign suggest about the American preoccupation with volunteerism and philanthropy? About its relationship to breast cancer as a charitable cause? And about the "character" debates in the NFL?

At one level, the Real Men Wear Pink campaign promoted an alternative version of masculinity—one that is sensitive, compassionate, and charitable—to that with which the NFL is more commonly associated. For a culture obsessed with role models and citizen education, the image of five professional football players who are suitably "diverse" and who are engaged in genuine and meaningful service to their fellow citizens was surely ideal. But, the Real Men Wear Pink campaign was also part of a discursive formation in which a player's character is judged, at least in part, on the basis of his involvement in philanthropy and volunteerism, and in which participation in these activities is articulated to good character and understood, like race, to be predictive of a player's propensity to crime. The character problem in the NFL, if we remember, was also blamed on the absence of a father figure in the players' childhoods. While anxieties about absent fathers are most obviously related to the alleged disintegration of the disciplinary mechanisms of the heteronormative nuclear family, these anxieties are linked, in important ways, to contemporary discourse on volunteerism and philanthropy.

Like the youth who were the target of Colin Powell's highly publicized volunteerism crusades in the 1990s, many NFL players grew up in households headed by a "welfare mother" and were thus, it is implied, deprived of "generous" and "independent" role models. In this context, it is notable that the official aim of the NFL-sponsored President's Summit on America's Future—the 1997 extravaganza at which Powell and then president Clinton launched their campaign to "make volunteerism part of the definition of citizenship"—was to provide two million underprivileged youth with "five fundamental resources" by the year 2000: mentors, adequate health care, safe places to go after school, job skills, and *the opportunity to do volunteer work.* Thus, the underprivileged youth who were to be the beneficiaries of the newly invigorated individual and corporate generosity that was to emerge from the summit were also to be trained *as* volunteers—trained to avoid, that is, the life choices taken by their implied and figurative parents, the "welfare queen" and the absent black father. In an era in which "neither the government nor the private sector can adequately address the needs of the nation's 15 million disadvantaged children," these children were to learn how to give as well as to receive, to become a generation of adults who are *not* dependent.[80]

In the context both of contemporary discourse on volunteerism and responsibility and the debate about character in the NFL, Real Men Wear Pink might best be read as an advertisement for the promise of personal, private philanthropy in the post–welfare reform era.[81] Because at the same time that the emergence of cause-related marketing is an *effect* of social developments associated with the rise of Reaganomics and neoliberalism in the United States, marketing strategies such as Real Men Wear Pink are also mechanisms for the production of ideals of citizenship.

The players who appear in these commercials, and whose participation in philanthropic and volunteer activity is the stuff of an endless stream of press releases, are the exemplars of "good character," where the latter is defined by a willingness to embrace bourgeois, humanistic values such as the need to perform organized, charitable works. The particular form of compassionate culture that the campaign represents and for which the "American people" are currently supposed to strive is one in which acts of organized volunteerism signify both concern for others and self-responsibility and fulfillment. However, this is most definitely *not* a culture that recognizes the informal networks of support and care upon which poor, urban, and rural communities often depend *as* (American) generosity.

At the same time that the Real Men Wear Pink Campaign offers a model for the ideal practitioner of American generosity, it also provides a model for the ideal recipient of volunteerism. Unlike the welfare queen—the quintessential antimother and the symbol of all that threatens the moral guardianship, selflessness, and good health on which nationally sanctioned motherhood depends—the breast cancer survivors we see in Real Men Wear Pink and in discourse on breast cancer more broadly are the embodiment of a white, middle-class, nationally sanctioned womanhood. As survivors, they are ordained with an inherent wisdom and morality. Through their participation in the Race they are at once recipients and purveyors of charity and bearers of the moral worth bound up with healthy discipline. Moreover, they appear as beacons of hope who, through their individual courage, strength, and vitality, have elicited an outpouring of American generosity, a continued supply of which will ensure that the fight against beast cancer remains an unqualified success.

The Future of Breast-Cancer-Related Marketing: Think Before You Pink?

Although breast-cancer-related marketing campaigns come and go (the Komen-NFL partnership, for instance, ended in 2001) and although the corporate interest in breast cancer seems as though it should have reached saturation point long ago, American businesses continue to produce new breast cancer campaigns and consumers continue to buy the goods with which these campaigns are associated. The outpouring, in other words, persists (in March 2005 alone, I came across a pair of snowshoes, a set of kitchen knives, and a rhinestone watch with a breast cancer theme).

It was in response to the continuous flow of breast-cancer-related products into the marketplace that Breast Cancer Action, the San Francisco–based activist group, created Think Before You Pink, urging consumers to "think twice before supporting the ubiquitous cause-related marketing pitches." The campaign was launched in 2002 with the placement of an advertisement in the *New York Times* during National Breast Cancer Awareness Month drawing attention to corporate "pinkwashers" who, in BCA's words, "exploit breast cancer to sell products."[82] An ad was placed in the same venue the following October, and there also exists a Web site explaining the issues the campaign seeks to address.[83]

Among the corporations targeted by Think Before You Pink are Avon, Eureka, American Express, Yoplait, and BMW. In each case, BCA highlights the minuscule amount of money that is actually raised through their respective marketing efforts and the generous amounts of publicity they receive in return. We are told, for instance, that American Express donates one penny per transaction at select vendors throughout October as part of its Charge for the Cure campaign. But, as BCA's Web site makes clear, a consumer would have to use his or her American Express card one hundred times in a thirty-one-day period in order to raise just one dollar for the cause. Similarly, BCA informs readers that Yoplait yogurt's Save Lids to Save Lives would require a person to eat three containers of yogurt every day over a four-month campaign to raise just thirty-six dollars for the Komen Foundation. In the case of BMW's Ultimate Drive campaign, in which the automaker donates one dollar to Komen for each mile anyone test-drives a car in the Ultimate Drive collection, BCA focuses on the polycyclic aromatic hydrocarbons present in car exhaust that have been linked to breast cancer and other illnesses.

The Think Before You Pink campaign has provoked extensive media coverage in outlets including *USA Today*, the *Wall Street Journal*, NBC, and CNN. Its success in drawing attention to the exploitative nature of much breast-cancer-related marketing, however, has been met by new tactics on the part of corporations and their nonprofit partners to ensure the health of this industry. Barbara Brenner, executive director of BCA, notes that her group was asked by the Komen Foundation to submit in advance all materials that were to be made available at their booth at the San Francisco Race for the Cure.[84] Although BCA is yet to find out exactly what led to this request, they learned from a newspaper reporter who was working on

Who's really cleaning up here?

It sounds noble: Buy this vacuum cleaner and Eureka will give a dollar to a breast cancer organization.

But wait. A dollar gift on a $200 purchase is less than one percent—and Eureka caps its annual contribution from the sales at $250,000.

Is the company spending more on its "Clean for the Cure" ads than it's donating to the cause?

It's not just Eureka. American Express donates a penny per transaction when you "Charge for the Cure." BMW kicks in a buck per mile when you test-drive its cars, which produce chemical compounds linked to breast cancer.

Avon lipstick, Yoplait yogurt—the list goes on and on. During Breast Cancer Awareness Month, pink-ribbon promotions are everywhere.

Breast Cancer Action urges you to "think before you pink." Will your purchase make a difference? Or is the company exploiting breast cancer to boost profits?

Preventing, curing, and guaranteeing quality treatment for breast cancer will require real change — and not the kind you carry in your pocket.

BREAST CANCER ACTION

55 New Montgomery St., Suite 323, San Francisco, CA 94105 • www.ThinkBeforeYouPink.org

Breast Cancer Action Think Before You Pink campaign poster, New York Times, *October 2002.*

THE COSMETICS INDUSTRY AND BREAST CANCER

Philanthropy
or Hypocrisy?

October is breast cancer awareness month, and major cosmetics companies—from Avon and Revlon to Estee Lauder—are marketing pink ribbon products to "support the fight against breast cancer."

That might seem like a good thing. But dozens of their products contain toxic ingredients that may be linked to breast cancer itself. Is this philanthropy? Or hypocrisy?

Parabens (PAIR-a-bens), used as preservatives, are endocrine disruptors that mimic the hormone estrogen. And increased estrogen exposure over a lifetime is a proven risk factor for breast cancer.

Phthalates (THAL-ates) help lotions penetrate the skin and make nail polish more flexible. They have been phased out of baby toys because of an association with birth defects and developmental disabilities. Because phthalates are also endocrine disruptors, concerns have been raised as well about their association with breast cancer.

With safer alternatives available, it's past time for the cosmetics giants to phase out these chemicals. In the meantime, they should be clearly listed on the label so consumers can make an informed choice.

After all, corporate conscience belongs in a company's products, not just its marketing.

To learn more about this issue, and what you can do about corporate "pinkwashing," visit www.ThinkBeforeYouPink.org.

☐ **I want to support this work.**

NAME   PHONE NUMBER

ADDRESS   E-MAIL ADDRESS

CITY   STATE   ZIP

Make checks payable to BCA and send to the address at right. Breast Cancer Action is a registered 501(c)3 nonprofit organization. Donations are tax-deductible to the extent provided by law.

BREAST CANCER ACTION

Breast Cancer Action
55 New Montgomery St., Suite 323
San Francisco, CA 94105

415-243-9301
Toll-free 877-2-STOP-BC (877-278-6722)

Breast Cancer Action Think Before You Pink campaign poster, New York Times, *October 2003.*

a feature story about Komen that the foundation viewed the Think Before You Pink campaign as directed toward them.

This point is also illustrated by BCA's long struggle to press the Avon corporation for accountability in the way it raises and spends the profits generated through its breast cancer fund-raising products and events.[85] In the summer of 2003, Avon began offering large grants ($200,000 over two years) to member organizations of Follow the Money: An Alliance for Accountability in Breast Cancer, a coalition of breast cancer activist groups spearheaded by Breast Cancer Action dedicated to tracking the money flooding into the breast cancer cause.[86] But their apparent generosity was accompanied by a nondisparagement clause that prevented recipients from criticizing Avon in any way. The Cancer Resource Center of Mendocino County was offered funds for its WeCAN program, which trains volunteers to assist women with breast cancer in rural northern California. According to Brenner, "CRCM was in no position to turn down the offered funds and accepted the gag order along with them." Likewise, the Babylon Breast Cancer Coalition (BBCC) was offered money, this time to channel toward environmental research, with the provision that the organization refrain from criticism of Avon and "be a positive presence at Avon's breast cancer walk." The coalition, however, unhappy with the conditions for the grants and by the failure of Avon to deal in good faith with the alliance in ongoing negotiations about how the funds raised by Avon's walk are spent (see chapter 2), declined Avon's offer. By Brenner's account, shortly after BBCC's rejection, Avon responded positively to requests for meetings with the alliance's allies in the socially responsible investment community to discuss further the issue of the use of potentially harmful chemicals in its products.[87]

Although BCA and BBCC's actions represent small dents in the armor of the breast cancer marketing industry, they are helping to shape a less certain future for businesses that for so long operated with impunity. BCA is also beginning to articulate to a wider audience their differences from large nonprofits such as the Komen Foundation. While criticizing—implicitly or explicitly—a fellow breast cancer organization clearly has its risks, in this particular case it may be the best solution. Although BCA denies with good reason that its Think Before You Pink campaign is targeted at the Komen Foundation, the breast-cancer-related marketing industry is as dependent on Komen as Komen is on its corporate partners, at least for as long as these corporations see profitability in an association with breast cancer. This is a synergistic relationship, in other words, that is best dealt with as such. As the Komen Foundation and its corporate partners continue to pump money into a research and education agenda that centers on uncritically promoting mammography, encouraging the use of pharmaceuticals to "prevent" breast cancer, and avoiding any consideration of environmental links to the disease, it becomes less clear whether or not they are actually doing more good than harm and whether, therefore, it is possible, or desirable, to avoid explicit criticisms of their activities.

Chapter 2

Doing Good
by Running Well

The Race for the Cure
and the Politics of Civic Fitness

*You get to feel good about yourself the whole time
because you're not only (selfishly) running to get fit but
you're (altruistically) helping others—you just can't beat
that deal.*
—Beth Hagman, *Fitness Runner* magazine

Since the mid-1980s, physical-activity-based fund-raising events (or "thons") for breast cancer have sprung up across the United States. In addition to the nation's largest series of 5K runs, the Susan G. Komen Breast Cancer Foundation's Race for the Cure, the dizzying array of challenges created by foundations and corporations include the American Cancer Society's Make Strides against Breast Cancer, a noncompetitive walk; the Danskin Women's Triathlon, which raises money for the Breast Cancer Research Foundation; the Revlon Run/Walk for Women (the second largest series of 5K events in the United States), which raises money in the name of "women's cancers" in general; the Avon Walk for Breast Cancer; the Climb to Fight Breast Cancer, the Climb for *a* Cure, and the Climb for *the* Cure, all of which take breast cancer survivors on mountaineering expeditions on some of the world's highest peaks; the Paddle for the Cure, a rowing event; the Ride for the Cure, a bicycle race; and the Breast Cancer 3-Day, a walk formerly organized by Avon in conjunction with Pallotta Teamworks and recently purchased by the Komen Foundation. In addition to this considerable range of activities, dragon boat racing for breast cancer survivors is growing at such an intense pace that both the U.S. Dragon Boat Federation and the International Dragon Boat Federation now include events exclusively for teams made up of women who have had the disease.

This chapter takes as its focus the oldest, most visible, and most profitable of breast cancer thons: the Race for the Cure. The Race for the Cure was first held in Dallas, Texas, in October 1983, when 700 participants took part. By 1999, the Race was the nation's largest 5K series, with events in ninety-nine cities across the United States. Between 1988 and 1999, participation in the series increased tenfold to nearly 600,000, grew by 44 percent between 1997 and 1998 alone, and reached 1.4 million in 2005. The National Race for the Cure, held in Washington, D.C., each June, is now the biggest 5K run in the world, according to the Race for the Cure Web site.

In addition to high rates of participation, the appeal of the Race for the Cure is apparent in its capacity to attract high-profile corporate sponsors, as well as the support and attendance of politicians and celebrities at events across the United States. Its stated purpose is to raise money for breast cancer research, screening, and education (the series raised $87,560,401 gross and $65,382,045 net in 2003, the most recent year for which figures are available) and to promote breast cancer awareness, particularly early detection. In the Komen Foundation's publicity materials and in mass media discourse, the Race is also configured as a mass-participation, authentically grassroots social movement that has succeeded in revolutionizing attitudes toward breast cancer and catapulting the disease to the top of the national biomedical research agenda.[1]

The Race for the Cure is a carefully orchestrated and centrally managed affair. Although organizers of individual races are permitted to inject a hint of local flavor into their events, an interview with a race organizer in the western United States revealed that the general format is determined by the foundation headquarters in Dallas so that one gathering is remarkably similar to the next: each event has a pre- and postrace rally, a survivor recognition ceremony, a "wellness" area, and a spot where corporate sponsors promote their wares. Race T-shirts, signage, and other publicity materials are all embossed with the foundation's logo, and there is a template for the signs, imprinted with the names of loved ones who have survived or died from breast cancer, that participants pin to their backs. Much of the music that blasts from the loudspeakers during the events is the same across the nation, and certain of the spoken passages from the pre- and postrace rallies are identical.

So although the main focus of this chapter is on field research conducted at one race and while the analysis is concerned in part with the specificities of this particular event, research at two other Race for the Cure events,

Komen Web site materials, and the aforementioned interview suggests that the Race for the Cure in any town or city across the United States will look very much the same.[2] The Race, in other words, has become a familiar and reliable brand, and its success is such that numerous corporations and foundations have attempted to reproduce the formula to raise money for their chosen causes. It is no longer the case that fund-raising walks begin with a few words of encouragement from a volunteer with a loudspeaker and a reflective vest and end with a pat on the back and a cup of water for each participant. Now huge rallies; rock-concert-sized stages; upbeat music; corporate sponsors; celebrity appearances; sophisticated signage; trademarked baseball caps, T-shirts, and water bottles; and formal recognition of survivors or other exemplars of the charity's good work are standard features of most events. The implications of this shift for the politics of breast cancer, for the cultural meanings of the thon and its potential as an organizing and educative tool, and for the broader civic culture of the United States are explored in the analysis that follows.

The National Race for the Cure

The Day's Events

On June 6, 1999, I traveled to Washington, D.C., to attend the Tenth Anniversary National Race for the Cure. Already the world's largest 5K event, the 1999 Race registered 65,000 runners and broke its own record for participation (52,000) set the previous year. Women with breast cancer and their colleagues, friends, and families traveled from all over the United States to take part, along with thousands of local residents from Maryland, Virginia, and the District itself. As with Race for the Cures across the country, many participants entered as members of sororities and fraternities or as employees running on corporate, government, diplomatic community, and voluntary sector teams.

While the race itself took runners through the streets of the capital, the rally site was located on the grounds of the Washington Monument, around which a huge area of grass and footpaths had been cordoned off. Immediately alongside the monument stood a 150-foot-tall bright pink, looped ribbon, the now ubiquitous representation of breast cancer charity and awareness in the United States. The rally stage was situated immediately in front of these monuments; its backdrop consisted of three enormous

Sunrise Survivor Celebration, National Race for the Cure, Washington, D.C., June 6, 1999.
Photograph by the author.

black-and-white panels adorned with the names of the Race's numerous corporate sponsors.[3]

The day's events began at 6:30 a.m. with the Sunrise Survivor Celebration. The recognition of breast cancer survivors is a central theme in Race for the Cures across the country. At each event a time is set aside in the program for a breast cancer survivors' ceremony; for many women it is the

Main stage backdrop, National Race for the Cure, Washington, D.C., June 6, 1999. Photograph by the author.

highlight of their day. The response of Nancy Statchen, a two-and-a-half-year survivor, is typical:

> The whole experience was so inspiring to me, the survivors, their strength and vitality. . . . A year and a half after diagnosis, this event was the first time that I openly proclaimed my membership in this club. And how proud I am—women, all these incredible women. After being confronted with this demon, carrying on, stronger than ever, committed to helping join the cause.[4]

At the National Race for the Cure, thousands of participants lined up and filed slowly into the survivors' tent, its entrance marked by a metal archway festooned with bright pink balloons, to help themselves to a "survivors' breakfast" laid on by various corporate sponsors. The breakfast was followed, at 7:30 a.m., by the Ten-Star Salute to Survivors Parade (a feature that is common to all Race for the Cure events) and the Pre-Race Rally.

Led by Komen Foundation founder Nancy Brinker, thousands of breast cancer survivors, all sporting bright pink visors and T-shirts to distinguish themselves from other participants, marched down from the tent toward the main stage. Clapping and dancing to the words and music of Gloria Gaynor's "I Will Survive" (which has become something of an anthem in the breast cancer movement), they moved along a pathway lined on either side by a cheering crowd of thousands, and the Washington Mall was trans-

Survivor breakfast, Race for the Cure, Tucson, Arizona, April 1, 2001. Photograph by the author.

formed into an immense sea of pink and white. As the music grew louder and the clapping more vigorous, this group of predominantly white, predominantly middle-aged women took their place on the stage, their arms outstretched in the air, waving in time with the music.[5]

Following a mass recital of the Pledge of Allegiance, Priscilla Mack, cochair of the National Race, introduced the survivors to the crowd: "I am very proud to be surrounded by a sea of faith. Each survivor has to dig down deep and fight for her life. We applaud you and we stand behind you." Mack then proceeded to ask women who had survived breast cancer for thirty years or more to wave their hands and "be recognized." A handful of women raised their hands. As she counted down through the years until she reached one, the hands increased in number.

Standing close to the stage, I couldn't help but recall Audre Lorde's well-known entry in *The Cancer Journals* when she points to "socially sanctioned prosthesis" as "another way of keeping women with breast cancer silent and separate from each other." Lorde then asks, "What would happen if an army of one-breasted women descended upon Congress and demanded that the use of carcinogenic, fat-stored hormones in beef-feed be outlawed?"[6] Here was an army of postmastectomy/lumpectomy women, assembled in the nation's capital, but surely not in a way that Lorde imagined.

This was an intensely moving moment, both for the survivors on the stage and the crowds on the mall, many of whom wore signs on their backs with the names of loved ones who had survived or died from breast cancer. For some women on the stage it was the first time that they had publicly declared their identity as breast cancer survivors (one woman I spoke to told me that it had taken her two years to pluck up the courage to attend the Race *as* a survivor). For others, the Race marked the first time that they had gone without a wig in public. Moreover, these women were far from silent and stood as a powerful symbol of the sheer number of people affected by the disease, as well as the possibility of triumph over illness. Proud, vibrant, hopeful, and passionate, clad in brightly colored athletic apparel, and participating in vigorous physical activity to raise money for a worthy

Sunrise Survivor Celebration, National Race for the Cure, Washington, D.C., June 6, 1999. Photograph by the author.

cause, these survivors seemed far removed from the alienated women with cancer of whom Lorde wrote so eloquently. Their self-presentation also contrasted starkly with the weak, pale, bedridden, cancer victim that has in prior decades stood as the dominant embodiment of the disease.

As commentators on the AIDS epidemic have argued, however, the deployment of positive images of disease raises complex political questions. While AIDS activists recognized early on the importance of challenging the hegemony of pessimistic, often hateful, images of people with AIDS and the pervasive rhetoric of the "AIDS victim," it was also the case that overly bright and hopeful configurations of the disease and of survivorship had the capacity both to undermine demands that the syndrome be taken seriously and to dissipate the rage of activists that was so crucial to sustaining the AIDS movement. Likewise, the highly orchestrated survivor celebrations that are central to the mission and appeal of the Race for the Cure highlight the individual strength, courage, and perseverance of women with breast cancer and offer an important source of hope and (albeit temporary) community, but they leave little room for the politically targeted anger that Lorde envisioned. The resulting rhetoric is so upbeat and so optimistic that it is possible to deduce from these events that breast cancer is a fully curable disease from which people no longer die.

At 8:30 a.m., buoyed by this intensely joyful atmosphere, the race began. Led by Al and Tipper Gore (the honorary race chairs) and numerous members of Congress, 65,000 runners, walkers, and wheelchair racers lined up on Constitution Avenue and moved slowly forward as they waited for their turn to cross the starting line. Many participants carried official placards emblazoned with the name of their team (such as "Bristol Myers Squibb," "AT&T," "Italy," "Myanmar," and "Bangladesh"). The master of ceremonies, to enthusiastic cheers from participants and spectators, called out these names as each team crossed the line. Their route took them along Constitution Avenue, around the U.S. capitol, on to Pennsylvania Avenue, and across the finish line at Federal Triangle. All along the way the sidewalks were packed with hundreds of cheering onlookers, volunteers, and stewards. As participants finished the race by crossing under yet another giant metal archway festooned with pink balloons, they were given bottles of Deer Park Spring Water, and all breast cancer survivors received a special medal donated by Bristol Myers Squibb Oncology.

Back on the grounds of the monument, sponsoring corporations set up tables from which to distribute "free stuff," including J. C. Penney water

bottles, National Football League key chains, and Ford Motor Company ban-
danas. Large numbers of people crowded around the stands with their hands
in the air, waiting to grab whatever goods were thrown their way. Participants
could also spend time in the Mosaic Women's Wellness Tent, in which an
array of hospitals, cancer clinics, health insurers, alternative treatment centers, pharmaceutical companies, and cancer support groups and charities had
tables with information advertising their products and services.

Cures and Corporations

During the pre- and postrace rallies, the crowd heard various speeches
from local celebrities, corporate CEOs (pharmaceutical companies that
sell cancer products were particularly prominent), Komen Foundation
members, and Al and Tipper Gore. We were also introduced to then sec-
retary of state Madeleine Albright and numerous members of Congress,
both Republicans and Democrats. The content of these speeches was overwhelmingly optimistic and focused predominantly on celebrating survivors
and reiterating the importance of cure-oriented science underwritten by
corporate support, generous individuals, and the Race for the Cure. Nancy
Brinker's hope-filled words were typical:

> Today is a defining moment in the breast cancer movement, because we are
> making progress. Twenty years ago, when my sister Susan Komen asked me
> to do something to cure this disease, we couldn't even imagine a day like
> today. Sixty-five thousand people turning out in our nation's capital to once
> again race, run, walk, and pray for the cure. It is coming! It is coming!

Although in media coverage and in Komen Foundation press releases,
the Race was framed as an opportunity to stress the importance of early
detection—via mammograms—in the fight against breast cancer, very
little was said (outside of the Women's Wellness Tent) about this during the
day's events. Instead, the focus was on reiterating the importance of science,
commerce, and good people with big hearts in the race to find a cure.

The Komen Foundation's focus on early detection and cure-oriented science has helped it win generous sponsorship from pharmaceutical companies, such as Zeneca and Bristol Myers Squibb, and mammography equipment and film manufacturers Du Pont and Kodak, all of which featured
prominently at the Race. A speech from a representative from Bristol Myers
Squibb Oncology (BMSO), for example, emphasized the corporation's

commitment to the cause and its faith in cure-oriented science: "We have come together to form a team to Race for the Cure. Bristol Myers Squibb continues to believe that by working as a team to raise awareness and fund research, a cure for this disease can and will be found."

The Komen Foundation's emphasis on finding a cure certainly articulates the Race to the national prestige bound up with the fight against cancer in a way that a focus on prevention, and all that it connotes, does not. That is, the search for a "magic bullet" (a specific treatment that will root out and destroy cancerous cells for good) channels research questions and public attention toward individual pathology or deviation from a biological norm and away from more difficult questions related to social conditions, environmental factors, and other "external" variables.[7] In this respect, the Komen Foundation is part of a long tradition: Faith in the power of positive thinking, the promotion of research into finding a cure for cancer above research focusing on prevention, and the belief that large infusions of money into research can conquer anything have been remarkably durable features of the various manifestations of the alliance against cancer in the twentieth century.[8]

The focus on finding a cure for breast cancer, rather than on prevention of the disease, has been subject to critique from some prominent scientists and breast cancer activists, however.[9] Many of these critics also express doubt about the usefulness of mammograms in the fight against cancer and point out, among other things, that even under optimal conditions, mammograms can miss up to 15 percent of tumors. They also argue that mammograms are not preventive but detective technologies and that the widespread promotion of this technology as preventive is deceptive and even dangerous, since some research suggests that overuse of mammograms might actually cause cancer. Furthermore, although early detection is touted by the breast cancer industry as increasing survival rates, critics have argued that while mammograms might detect tumors earlier they do not necessarily improve the survival of patients, but rather extend the amount of time in which women bear knowledge of their condition. In other words, this technology may have very little impact on overall breast cancer mortality.

Consumer-Citizens

Reflecting on the postwar emergence of neoliberal political thought, Nikolas Rose has argued that in recent decades self-gratification is no longer defined in opposition to civility, as it was in the ethical codes of puritan sects that Max Weber considered so important in the early moments of capitalism.[10] Consumers, that is, can—and do—build civic identity and virtue through their consumption practices. And since the 1990s, as we saw in the previous chapter, corporations have done the same. They produce goods for profit and promote these goods by aligning themselves with virtuous causes. While members of the cancer industries were given a particularly prominent role at the race, corporations in general emerged as exemplary citizens in the course of the day's events. Drawing attention to the names of businesses emblazoned on the stage backdrop and on the official race T-shirts, National Race for the Cure executive cochair Mack declared, "With sponsors like these, we will find a cure!" Similarly, the volunteer coordinator for the Komen Foundation told the cheering crowd, "When you think volunteerism, you think reach out and touch someone and I just love that model. That model is the corporate logo of AT&T and they're a national leader in volunteerism."

Commodities such as the Race for the Cure (you pay in exchange for the opportunity to participate, an official T-shirt, and "freebies" that vary with each race) also appear to illuminate or reveal the virtuosity of those who buy them, to transform purchasers into certain kinds of people living certain kinds of lives. Thus, the National Race for the Cure might be understood as a site for the production of both consumer-citizens and corporate citizens and as such exemplifies the ways in which citizenship advances through consumption at this particular moment in history.

In this context, perhaps the most interesting speech of the day came from Rae Evans, a longtime Washington lobbyist, corporate strategist, and founding member of the National Race for the Cure.[11] Evans began her address by (mis)quoting Martin Luther King's most famous words. She said:

> About thirty years ago, the Reverend Martin Luther King stood on this hallowed ground and echoed the phrase "I have a dream." "I have a dream," he said, "*for girls and boys of all colors and shapes and sizes to walk together.*" I'm here today . . . to share with you and tell you that Gretchen Poston and Susan Komen had a dream too. That dream is realized today by your presence, by your support, and by your enthusiasm. (Emphasis added)[12]

Although Evans's misquote reveals, perhaps, as much about the incorporation of the image and legacy of Martin Luther King during this period as it does about the Race for the Cure, there is a way in which these two events are related. Scholars of race have taught us to recognize the ways that narratives such as this are structured by a discourse of whiteness, characterized by a muted and often awkward racial awareness that operates alongside a "color" and "power evasiveness" (to use Ruth Frankenberg's terms).[13] Here Evans's words display just this type of ambivalence. A brief gesture is made to recognize King, the most prominent symbol of civil rights organizing and race consciousness in the United States, but this gesture is swiftly undercut by the erasure of terms that signify violence and inequality (e.g., "vicious racists") and that make race visible (e.g., "little black boys" and "little white girls"). Evans draws, in other words, on the "moral language of the collectivism of the African American struggle for civil rights," even though the actual content of the Race for the Cure and the overall agenda of the Komen Foundation is largely individualistic.[14] She references the King speech while employees and volunteers of the organization and attendees at events like the Race for the Cure are overwhelmingly white. And she mobilizes this discourse despite the fact that the Komen Foundation steers clear of social-justice-oriented breast cancer work and at certain moments has actively opposed measures that might benefit the marginalized and oppressed.[15]

In transforming the content of King's speech from a concern with violent racism, injustice, and deep-seated inequalities into a lesson about body shape, size, and image, Evans also demonstrates how we rewrite and re-create the past in order to forge a more palatable present. Her words indicate how the Race for the Cure has become one among many tools for the rewriting of history and for the transformation of the public sphere, politics, and citizenship in the present. Lauren Berlant argues that press reports of the thirtieth anniversary of Martin Luther King's March on Washington sanitized an event that in 1963 created panic and threats of racist counter-violence. In retrospect the event was transformed into a "beautifully choreographed mass rationality, an auteurist production of the eloquent, rhetorically masterful, and then martyred King."[16] The sanitization of the King speech and march, therefore, is also a symptom of nostalgia for a time when protest was apparently more reasonable and orderly.

In the past two decades, conflict and dissent have been typically portrayed by the mainstream media as passions that are dangerous and destabilizing. By focusing on the most disorderly performances of resistance, the media have cast public activism (on both the left and the right) as naive, ridiculous, shallow, and juvenile. Protest is, to paraphrase Berlant, doubly humiliated, both silly and dangerous. The media subtract personhood from activists, making their practices of citizenship seem proof that their very claims are illegitimate. In contrast, talk shows and other forms of gossip media have helped

make personal witnessing about trauma or injury highly valued political tes-
timony. The stories of breast cancer survivorship recited at the Race for the
Cure, like those that characterize these popular media genres, use sentimen-
tality to elicit personal identification with abstract and difficult issues. The
Race for the Cure has become, in other words, part of a discursive formation
that contributes to the widely held assumption that the only way Americans
can claim both rights and mass sympathy is to demonstrate not panic or anger
but ethical serenity, patriotism, and proper deference.[17]

Indeed, anger, dissent, or criticism of any kind were stark in their absence
at the National Race for the Cure. No questions were asked about, nor was
there any mention of, persistently high rates of breast cancer in the United
States and worldwide. Although the participation of thousands of survivors
should be indicative of these rates, their presence was celebrated as evidence
of the promise of individual struggle against the disease rather than of a crisis that kills forty thousand women in the United States alone each year.
Survivors, in other words, stood as symbols of hope for the future, rather
than of urgency in the present. Differences of age, race, and class in mortality rates were also ignored or subsumed under the banner of the "survivor."
Moreover, no demands for action, beyond calls for continued participation in
the Race for the Cure, were made of the various representatives of the cancer
industries or the state, nor indeed of participants in the Race.

It could be argued, of course, that the Race for the Cure is designed to
raise money (more than two million dollars, in this instance) and celebrate
survivorship, not to provide a platform for the expression of dissent that
Audre Lorde had envisioned. It could also be argued that there is a place for
such celebratory and harmonious public gatherings. But to do so would be
to ignore the implication of the Race in a broader war of position over what
constitutes "the problem of breast cancer" in the present moment and over
what kinds of actions and identities are legitimate or effective in bringing
about social change. It would be to disregard, in other words, how the Race
works to legitimate particular forms of publicity and participation at the
same time that it helps to marginalize others.

The Ribbon and the Monument; or, The Politics of Innocence

The pairing of the giant pink ribbon with the Washington Monument
presents a particularly rich symbolic setting through which to think about
the articulation of breast cancer philanthropy to contemporary ideals of

The Washington Mall, National Race for the Cure, Washington, D.C., June 6, 1999. Photograph by the author.

national identity, prestige, and citizenship. For although the Washington Mall is the site of a rather circumscribed narrative of citizenship and nationalism with its pristine white monuments and "great man" statues, it is also a primary location for national protest. The Mall is most usefully understood, therefore, as an index of American history: the celebrations and demonstrations that take place in its shadow are events that both reflect and reproduce particular periods and versions of the nation's history.[18] Thus, the positioning of the ribbon alongside the monument—a place of tribute to the nation's founder, an emblem of freedom and justice, and the most symbolic national locale of the United States—helps establish the Race in particular, and breast cancer fund-raising more generally, as sites through which contemporary versions of "America" and American citizenship are enacted.

The ribbon and the monument, side by side, might be understood to represent a partnership between the nation-state, the nonprofit sector, and the corporate world (for whom the pink ribbon has become a staple of cause-related marketing). In this formulation, the ribbon symbolizes both grassroots and corporate activism, and the monument, the nation-state, willing to listen and representative of the needs and desires of its people; both structures stand as powerful symbols of America the free, just, and virtuous nation. The ribbon—pink and round, feminine and innocent, a national emblem of "awareness" and good, sensible, consumption-based citizenship—represents an ideal partner to the strong, yet compassionate and accommodating, nation-state. Together they stand as a quintessential signifier for the post-welfare-reform era in which well-intentioned, charitable individuals must share the burden of governing and the fulfillment of their needs with the state, the market, and the nonprofit sector.

The "innocence" of the pink ribbon is worth dwelling on here. Breast cancer fund-raising organizations and events have helped shape the meaning of the ribbon as a symbol of innocence and unquestionably good intention in order to elicit identification and support for their cause. But Barbara Christian reminds us that innocence has a dual meaning: to be innocent is to be prepolitical (as in the innocence of childhood), but to be innocent is also to *refuse to know*.[19] She goes on to argue that innocence in this respect is unethical and constitutive of weak citizenship. Yet it is precisely a refusal to know that has itself been taken up as an ethical practice in the government of the self in the latter part of the twentieth century and beyond. This is not to suggest that the era in which we live is marked by a refusal to know, period, but rather that it is characterized by a shift in the appropriate *focus* for knowing. In the age of "intimate citizenship" (Berlant's term), in which politics via mass anger and disruption is dismissed as silly, dangerous, and futile, an ethic of self-government has emerged that encourages people to turn their critical selves inward and to question and work upon their psychic health and self-esteem. Individual fulfillment and an ethical life are to be achieved through these styles of self-management, as well as through the work that individuals do in their communities. But being an active, virtuous, and "community-minded" citizen does not mean starting with a view of the United States as a site of struggle acutely divided along axes of race, sex, and class and in need of ongoing social transformation. Instead, the preferred ideal is to know and work upon one's self and one's community through personal acts of philanthropy and unpaid service to one's fellow citizens in a space that is imagined to be outside of the realm of social inequality and political struggle. It is the existence of this ideal, moreover, alongside the good intentions and apparent harmlessness of these practices that makes this formation so hard to contest.

Writing on what she views as the decline of the American public sphere, Berlant claims that there is no public sphere in the contemporary United States, no context of communication and debate that makes ordinary citizens feel they have a common culture or influence on a state that holds itself accountable to their opinions, critical or otherwise. She argues that the antiwar, antiracist, and feminist agitations of the 1960s, which denounced the "hollow promises of the pseudopublic sphere," have been demonized by a conservative coalition whose aim was the privatization of U.S. citizenship.[20] Accordingly, the critical energies of the emerging political sphere have been rerouted into the sentimental spaces of opinion culture, characterized by antistatist, antifederalist, yet patriotic identification mixed with feelings of political powerlessness. The marketing of nostalgic images of a normal, familial America that have come to define the utopian and appropriate context for citizen aspiration is central to this shift. Berlant claims that from these transformations has emerged an intimate public sphere in which citizenship is rendered as a condition of social membership produced by personal acts and values, especially acts originating in or directed to the family sphere.[21]

Mass media accounts of the Race for the Cure and the speeches given at the Washington event route identification with breast cancer as a cause, and with the Komen Foundation particularly, through traditional and nostalgic notions of the home, family, and community. At the National Race, the president of the federal mortgage guarantee company Freddie Mac told the crowd that the race was about the "well-being of the nation's families." Deploying language with strong echoes of the eugenicist discourse that was so prominent in early-twentieth-century thinking about race and reproduction, he continued, "Healthy mothers and daughters," he said, "mean healthier families and happier homes." Thus, American motherhood and family must be protected from a disease that threatens not just individual lives but also the normalized socioeconomic identities and relationships that constitute the nuclear family. This discourse of American family does not simply refer to the literal effect of sickness and death on family relationships, however. Rather, it both stems from and helps reinforce the link between the breast, motherhood, and nurturing, with the breast symbolizing both the nourishment and sustenance given to the child through breast-feeding and the social work of nurturing and mothering. In contrast, in media coverage of men with breast cancer, their suffering is *disarticulated* from femininity and the well-being of the nation's homes and families and *rearticulated* to concerns about the potential effects of the disease on their masculinity.

Mass volunteerism and philanthropy through events like the Race for the Cure have become so successful partly because of their articulation to "the family," but also because they offer large groups of people the feeling that they *can* make a difference. Since 1992, there has been an enormous increase in federal dollars for breast cancer research and extensive coverage of events such as National Breast Cancer Awareness Month. Thus, whatever critics might think of the kinds of change that have been won or the way the money has been spent, participants in events such as Race for the Cure can see the tangible effects of their participation and their impact on the state. Moreover, the presence of numerous representatives of the state and of corporate America at the National Race legitimates the particular forms of citizenship enacted there. Thus, to note that visible dissent was absent from the National Race for the Cure is not to suggest that this event is somehow "apolitical." Rather, what we are witnessing here is a transformation and reconstitution of the political through mass participation in events such as Race for the Cure, and the emergence of an ethicopolitics of self-fulfillment and community action through volunteerism and philanthropy more generally.

The irony of the turn to volunteerism and philanthropy at the moment at which big government was declared to be at an end is, in the case of breast cancer at least, that it is precisely such individualistic, yet public, forms of volunteerism that have brought the state further into the funding and regulation of the breast cancer industry. In this respect, the Komen Foundation and the Race for the Cure might be read as quintessential tools of neoliberal governmentality.[22] While the Komen Foundation refuses to hold the state responsible for guaranteeing certain rights and needs to its citizens in the form of access to health care (Mary Ann Swissler's research reveals that the Komen Foundation lobbied against the consumer-friendly version of the Patients' Bill of Rights in 1999, 2000, and 2001 and worked in support of George W. Bush's corporate-friendly proposal in 2001), it is committed to the state as a crucial vehicle in the "elusive search for a cure" and for creating and maintaining the conditions in which free enterprise (individual and corporate) and the market for breast cancer can flourish.[23]

Moreover, the willingness of the state to intervene and the seemingly universal acknowledgment that such intervention is a good thing suggest that it is the meanings, values, and political subjects associated with the breast cancer movement that make women with breast cancer legitimate dependents on the state. It is not simply the absence of a sense of collective, political struggle from the Race for the Cure that deems it a site for the production of virtuous citizens, then, but also its emphasis on moral worth via individual responsibility and proper consumption. That is, by promoting early detection, consumption of Kellogg's Wheat Bran Flakes, regular exercise, and volunteerism, the Race for the Cure, and discourse on breast cancer more broadly, works as a technique for the production of self-responsible consumer-citizens.

American Fitness: The Rise of the Thon

The contemporary association of moral worth with both individual responsibility (particularly for one's health and bodily maintenance) and participation in volunteerism is exemplified in the recent proliferation of "thons." In the present moment, it is virtually unheard of for a participatory sports event not to be linked to a charitable cause, and breast cancer foundations are among the most popular of the chosen beneficiaries. But beyond breast cancer nonprofits, almost all the major health charities organize national networks of exercise-based events, and many smaller organizations, both health-related and otherwise, do the same. The American Cancer Society runs the Relay for Life (est. 1985) and Making Strides against Breast Cancer (est. 1993; the only disease-specific thon sponsored by the society); the American Heart Association organizes Jump Rope for Heart (est. 1979) and Hoops for Heart (est. 1992–93); the American Lung Association stages the Big Ride across America (est. 1998); the Leukemia and Lymphoma Society puts on Team in Training (est. 1988); the March of Dimes hosts one of the oldest thons, WalkAmerica (est. 1970); and various AIDS service organizations and foundations across the United States host long-distance bike rides and walks.

The present-day focus of these events on health within a strictly domestic context, however, is quite far removed from their historical roots, which were entangled with the struggle to forge international cooperation in the post–World War II era and with issues of "third world" development. During the 1950s, in response to high rates of poverty and malnutrition throughout the world, but especially in developing countries, the Food and Agricultural Organization of the United Nations launched the International Freedom from Hunger Campaign. As part of this operation, member nations were asked to form National Committees of the Freedom from Hunger Campaign. In Western Europe, these Committees launched the Walk for Development, in which individual participants were asked to generate pledges, as a strategy to raise money and public awareness of poverty and malnutrition. Eventually the idea for the walks spread to Canada, and in 1961 President John F. Kennedy's call for the development of youth leadership led to the establishment of an American affiliate, the American Freedom from Hunger Foundation (AFFHF).[24]

The AFFHF's mission was to encourage volunteerism and educate the American public about issues surrounding hunger. The AFFHF staged its first Walk for Development in 1968, and within a year a hundred walks had raised over $800,000 and involved more than half a million people in sixteen states across the United States. Between 1969 and 1970, four hundred walks raised a further half million dollars and gained front-page attention in the *New York Times* and *Reader's Digest*.[25] The Walks for Development had three main purposes: to raise funds for international development, to educate the public about the causes and effects of poverty and malnutrition, and to develop youth leadership (young people from junior high school through college organized the walks). According to former AFFHF officer Michael Seltzer, Hunger Hikes and Walks for Development were in many ways different from the thons of today. Operating under a donor choice format, the money raised often went to controversial causes such as National Welfare Rights and the American Indian Movement, and their public education often included radical critiques of structural inequality, racism, and colonialism. In addition, these walks were the means through which many youth became connected to the anti–Vietnam War movement.

Seltzer claims that the professionalization and marketization of fundraising events was the driving force in the gradual dissolution of Hunger

Hikes and Walks for Development. The March of Dimes was the first to copy the idea when in 1970 it launched its first walkathons (in San Antonio, Texas, and Columbus, Ohio), now known as WalkAmerica. Although walkathons became increasingly common through the 1970s, it was not until the mid-1980s and the emergence of the "fitness boom" that other exercise-based events proliferated.

The "fitness boom" is the term used to describe the turn to physical activity on the part of millions of previously sedentary, mostly middle- and upper-class, Americans and the concomitant appearance of numerous new fitness-related products on the market. Not coincidentally, the boom emerged at the same time that advanced capitalist technologies and the movement of manufacturing bases from the United States were exacting a devastating impact on the nation's poor and working class. The Reagan administration's response to elevated unemployment and poverty is by now familiar. With considerable assistance from the mass media, the government, in conjunction with the New Right and the Religious Right, engineered a national fantasy by which the effects of economic and social conditions (poverty and welfare "dependency") were blamed on individual inadequacies or failings and the breakdown of the family. As scholars of this era have suggested, the "national preoccupation with the body" (Alan Ingham's term), the rise of lifestyle politics, and the fitness boom can be understood both as ways to circumvent anxieties about the crisis of the "welfare state" and the family *and* as appeals to and celebrations of individualism and free will that were so central to the logic of Reaganism.[26]

As individuals were asked to take responsibility for their well-being and improve the quality of their lives, the film industry bombarded the American public with images promoting the hard and disciplined body, the marketing strategies of apparel companies like Nike and Reebok captured national attention, the figure of Rambo became an icon of national self-esteem, and an ever-growing army of TV fitness gurus "stepped" into our living rooms.[27] In sum, the ethos of self-betterment and quality of life through consumption became the normative code of conduct—and therefore that by which bodies were judged, celebrated, or condemned—for everyday life in America.[28]

Whereas in prior decades, fitness had been associated variously with anticommunism, crises of masculinity, and competitive sport, in the 1980s the fit body became at once a status symbol and an emblem of an individual's purchasing power, moral health, self-control, and personal discipline. This relationship, induced by the marketing and consumption of fitness products, was, moreover, a strategy of neoliberal governmentality. Individuals were encouraged, rewarded, and penalized for adopting, or failing to adopt, strategies for biological self-betterment by networks of government that sought to reduce health costs by educating the public against bodily neglect or abuse and by promoting the body as a locus of pleasure, self-expression, and personal fulfillment.[29]

The rapid growth and popularity of the highly commodified, individualistic fitness-based fund-raising activities such as the Race for the Cure, therefore, has been shaped by the consumer imperatives and normalizing logic of the fitness boom. In the present moment, participation in regular exercise has come to constitute a sign of proper citizenship at the same time that the source and the responsibility for one's health are increasingly understood to rest with individual lifestyle choices. Moreover, these social norms have coincided with an intensified interest in, and use of, volunteerism and philanthropy as modes of governance.

This is not to suggest that the technologies of the self encouraged by and reflected in the contemporary thon remain unchanged since the Reagan era. Instead, the thon appears to be bound up with a specifically post-1980s, post-yuppie antimaterialism that emerged in the 1990s and that claims that people "need to find fulfillment by giving to others" and that "just being rich doesn't quite cut it anymore." At the present time, the mass media pay considerable attention to the giving practices of both the very wealthy and the "average American." In these narratives (which tend not to extend their critique to questions of corporate tax breaks, deep-seated inequalities of income, or other girdles of global capitalism), massive accumulation of wealth accompanied by what is perceived as inadequate giving is condemned as crass and greedy, and the national character and spirit of America is judged on the grounds of the giving practices of its middle-class and wealthy citizens. In a similar vein, to exercise solely for one's own pleasure or health or for purely aesthetic ends is framed as narcissistic.

In an article for *Runner's World,* for instance, Lisa Hamm-Greenawalt, a competitive runner, described how she had entered her first Race for the Cure because she "wanted to try and run a strong 5K race" in order to launch her racing season. But, as Hamm-Greenawalt took her place at the starting line, it "finally dawned on" her that "this race meant a lot more than PR." Her mother had died of breast cancer six years previously, and she describes the anger she felt at herself for not wearing a sign "in memory of mom," for not finding sponsors to raise money, and for not "doing more" for the cause. Hamm-Greenawalt frames her experience as a parable about self-absorption, enlightenment, and redemption. She concludes the piece with a promise to "bring a different attitude to the event" in the following year by recruiting participants and declares, "Instead of focusing on PRs [personal records], I'll use the Race for the Cure to focus on joining my sisters to combat this cancer that has robbed us of too much, this killer that puts our own lives in danger."[30]

In contrast to the elitist charity galas of the upper classes, thons are commonly represented in media discourse as "athletic grassroots events" that are accessible and affordable. For instance, Patricia Cesar, vice president of Cesar & Washburn, a management and development consulting firm for foundations and nonprofit organizations, told the *New York Times:* "The walks also open up your ranks of supporters of your organization. It's a way to get everyone involved: celebrities, adults, children, families. Besides, people are tired of the $500-a-plate rubber chicken dinners, and these marathon events have inspired a whole new way of giving."[31] In a similar vein, Marty Liquori, former elite middle-distance runner and the national chairman of the Leukemia Society's marathon training program (which raised $38 million in 1998), told the same journalist, "It also gives those who can't make a financial contribution an opportunity to make a contribution of their time."[32] Although the piece omits to note that most of these events charge an entrance fee, which in the case of the Race for the Cure stands at between twenty-five and thirty dollars.

In an interview with the *Chicago Tribune,* Nancy Brinker, founder of the Komen Foundation, discussed her reasons for using a race to raise money and awareness:

> Sports events were becoming very big in the early '80s. People were focusing on fitness, and I felt that there was so much fear associated with even discussing this disease that we had to create an environment that was fun, that was uplifting, that was empowering.[33]

Brinker's idea was to "make people feel a sense of community and be able to share their fears and whatever they were feeling." When only seven hundred people turned out for the first race in Dallas in 1983, several people tried to convince Brinker that the event did not have growth potential and that she should continue with the more traditional events that were raising money. "But," Brinker said, "they weren't reaching the masses of people and they weren't providing education or helping to build a grass-roots organization so we could have a real political impact some day and get some money for research."[34]

Understood as vehicles for civic engagement and vital tools in grass-roots efforts to improve American society, thons are also portrayed as the antithesis of forms of participation understood to be alienating or imper-sonal. Many charities, for example, offer the opportunity for participants to express or forge personal connections to people with disease. As part of the Leukemia and Lymphoma Society's Team in Training program, run-ners are paired with one or more leukemia patients and wear wristbands bearing their names during the race. As *Fitness Runner* put it, "You're not just running for research and education. You're running for somebody. . . . Many participants get to know their Honored Patient, and more than one has said that gets them across the finish line."[35] Similarly, in the Race for the Cure, participants wear pink signs on their backs with the names of either breast cancer survivors or loved ones lost to breast cancer.

And because of the physical nature of the thon, participation is under-stood to be more proactive, even activist, than "simply" donating money. "The days of sitting back writing a check and sending it to a post office box or going door to door with a canister are bygone," said Dwayne Howell, president of the Leukemia Society of America.[36] One of my interviewees, a fifty-one-year-old army officer and breast cancer survivor, shared similar sentiments:

> It gives people a way to actively show their support to find a cure. When a person just donates money through the mail, they are unable to "touch" the results of their contribution. With the race, the supporters can be right there with the survivors who represent the positive aspects of their support through contributions. They can see the result of the research and new drugs— mothers, grandmothers, and daughters who are still alive to share memories with their families.[37]

As a practice that both elicits and shapes the physical, moral, and civic capacities of its participants, the Race for the Cure is an ideal tool for the production of proper citizens. Given that the success of any particular thon is measured by its capacity to gain individual physical commitment from its participants, who in turn must secure individual promises to donate money, it is not surprising that the thon emerged as a new site for mass public par-ticipation in the 1990s, a decade that witnessed the production of a con-stant flow of techniques, tools, and strategies designed to elicit individual responsibility and responsibility to others mediated not through the state but through the "freedom" of personal philanthropy and volunteerism.

In the specific context of the Race for the Cure, we can see how personal generosity comes to be mobilized and deployed as a form of collective, political action even as the event shuns struggle, debate, or critique of dominant social and economic relations and forces. In this respect, the Race has played an active role in shaping a social context that views "America's" survival as depending on personal acts of generosity mediated through consumer culture and in which it has become increasingly difficult to distinguish those activities that might help bring about social change from those that help to reproduce the status quo.

The Emergence of Dissent

It is precisely this type of confusion that has prompted a growing number of people to question the political and financial value of physical-activity-based fund-raising events. Fund-raising experts claim that thons have become popular not so much because of their money-making potential (often funds raised through thons make up only a small percentage of any organization's annual income, although the Race for the Cure is an exception here), but because of the publicity they generate for the foundations that sponsor them. For this reason, some nonprofit organizations have come under criticism from activist groups, notably those involved in the struggle against HIV/AIDS and breast cancer, for misleading participants about the fund-raising capacity of thons and for sinking money into the overhead expenditures for these flashy and costly spectacles rather than channeling it directly to the causes they support. There is, in other words, an emerging pattern of organized resistance to these events.

Breast Cancer Action (BCA) has been the most prominent voice of resistance, focusing its efforts, in particular, on the Avon corporation's breast cancer fund-raising events.[38] The company's inaugural Avon Breast Cancer 3-Day, a sixty-mile walk from Los Angeles to Santa Barbara, took place in 1998, and it was soon after that BCA began to express its concerns. Produced by Pallotta Teamworks, the controversial for-profit firm that created the now defunct AIDS Ride, the walk had grown to thirteen cities by 2002. The format for these walks is similar to the Race for the Cure, with inspirational ceremonies at either end of the event; wellness areas; pit stops for snacks and drinks, and toilets along the route; and booths for corporate sponsors. But in addition, the organizers provide overnight accommodation in the form of a tent village, as well as hot meals, showers, and nightly entertainment. With these kinds of undertakings, the cost of staging such events is considerable. Participants in the first Los Angeles walk, for instance, raised $7.79 million, of which only $5.02 million, or 64 percent of the total, went toward breast cancer organizations, with the remainder dedicated to administrative (including the producer's fee) and marketing expenses.[39]

It was in response to these figures, in addition to a number of other issues discussed below, that BCA first began raising its concerns. The campaign that resulted, Think Twice Before You Walk, fell under the rubric of a larger effort to track the money flooding into the breast cancer cause. This larger effort would eventually grow to comprise eleven breast cancer organizations across the United States and would come to be called Follow the Money: An Alliance for Accountability in Breast Cancer.

Writing in a 2000 BCA newsletter, the organization's executive director, Barbara Brenner, asked, "Whether you are a walker asking for pledges or a person who has pledged funds to support a walker, wouldn't it make far more sense to give your dollars directly to the breast cancer organizations you want to support?" In addition, Brenner noted that because each walker had to raise a minimum of $1,750 to participate *and* be in possession of health insurance, the walks were open to only the most privileged members of society. She also questioned how the money was spent. At this time Avon distributed the net proceeds to NABCO, which, in exchange for a fee, distributed the remaining funds to organizations promoting "breast health" awareness for underserved women. As Brenner pointed out, none of the funds could be used for actual screening and none could be used for treatment if these underserved women discovered they had breast cancer.[40]

As part of its effort, BCA conducted a letter-writing campaign to newspapers in the cities in which the walk was taking place. They also composed a template for a letter declining a request for a donation that concerned individuals could give to friends and acquaintances who were soliciting support for their participation in an Avon event. Eighteen months into the campaign, in October 2001, BCA convened a meeting between leaders of the Avon Products Foundation and activists from the Massachusetts Breast Cancer Coalition, the New York State Breast Cancer Alert, the New Jersey–based organization After Breast Cancer Surgery, and BCA itself. The activists made several suggestions for changes that could be made to the company's efforts in order to increase their effectiveness and "to build on the considerable public goodwill that already exists around the walks."[41] These changes included urging Avon to underwrite the administrative costs of the walks, to establish and rely on community service boards in deciding which breast cancer programs to fund in the geographic areas in which the walks were held, and to fund research projects and organizations that focus on prevention, rather than those that already receive substantial support from taxpayer-funded institutions and private interests. (In 2001, Avon awarded a $20 million grant to the National Cancer Institute, a taxpayer-funded agency that in 2000 received $582 million more in federal funding than agency leaders had requested from Congress.)[42]

In a BCA newsletter the following August, Brenner noted that the group's initial optimism after its meeting with Avon representatives was followed by "months of silence from Avon Foundation management."[43] So the alliance of organizations seeking to follow the money tried new approaches that included contacting Andrea Jung, Avon Products CEO; educating Avon shareholders (they focused in particular on asset management companies and mutual funds that practice socially responsible investing); and purchasing Avon stocks so that they could participate in shareholder meetings. These efforts clearly had an effect: in response to a question from an alliance member at the annual shareholder meeting in May, Jung announced that after 2002 Avon would not renew its contract with Pallotta Teamworks; shortly after the meeting, in June 2002, Avon announced that it would no longer sponsor its three-day walks but would instead investigate "new fundraising vehicles."[44] Soon thereafter, the company revealed that it would host its own series of Avon Walks for Breast Cancer (which would be two days long, rather than three) in eight cities the following year.[45] Although in the first two years of their existence these walks attracted smaller crowds than they had in their previous incarnation, eight walks were staged in 2005 and in 2006.

Soon after Avon severed its ties with Pallotta, the company closed its doors and declared bankruptcy. While the alliance noted that it was glad to see the end of the Avon partnership with Pallotta, they were, in the words of Brenner, "disheartened to hear that the corporation was abandoning this huge fundraising vehicle altogether." She went on to write: "The decision, however, reflects the essential nature of cause marketing. As long as 'doing good' doesn't have costs associated with it, corporations are more than happy to reap the benefits of their perceived largess."[46]

Opening ceremony, Avon Walk for Breast Cancer, Boston, May 15, 2004. Photograph by the author.

Opening ceremony, Avon Walk for Breast Cancer, Boston, May 15, 2004. Photograph by Jennifer Scott.

Writing messages on memorial column, Avon Walk for Breast Cancer, Boston, May 15, 2004. Photograph by the author.

This sequence of events, nevertheless, marked the end of Pallotta in name only. A few months later, the Komen Foundation began circulating advertisements for a three-day breast cancer walk that looked remarkably similar to publicity that Avon once used for its events; indeed, the logo was practically identical. The Komen Foundation, it turns out, had bought

Closing ceremony, Avon Walk for Breast Cancer, Boston, May 16, 2004. Photograph by the author.

Pallotta's assets and hired former Pallotta employees—who had managed to obtain the rights to the 3-Day logo—to produce its new venture. In 2003, former Pallotta employees also took their trade to Canada, where they established, in conjunction with the Princess Margaret Hospital in Toronto, the Weekend to End Breast Cancer. The new company is known as CauseForce—"one of the leading international producers of large-scale fundraising events"—and in 2006 it staged walks in six additional Canadian cities. In the same year, CauseForce introduced the format to England, where it produced the Aviva Weekend to Breakthrough Breast Cancer in London and Birmingham.[47]

This series of transactions, from Avon's decision to leave Pallotta but to keep the walk, to the Komen Foundation's decision to buy Pallotta's assets and establish a rival walk (when it already hosts a major series of events), to the movement of the template to new national markets, further highlights the extent to which fund-raising for breast cancer has become a highly valued commodity *in itself.* They demonstrate, in other words, how fund-raising for breast cancer has developed into a highly competitive market in which large foundations and corporations compete with one another to attract the loyalty of consumers who in this case are

The Susan G. Komen Breast Cancer 3-Day logo, "Changing Lives: The Breast Cancer 3-Day," Susan G. Komen Breast Cancer Foundation promotional pamphlet (Chicago: Breast Cancer Foundation, 2004).

well-intentioned members of the public who wish to do their part in the fight against the disease.

In addition to opening themselves up to charges of exploiting public goodwill and using it to support an agenda for breast cancer that is ultimately conservative, these large organizations and their fund-raising spectacles are deleteriously affecting the work that smaller advocacy groups can perform.[48] Thus, in a situation that is somewhat analogous to the effect of stores such as Wal-Mart and Target on small business owners, organizations such as Avon and the Komen Foundation are competing for donor-participants with smaller, community-based organizations,

*The Avon Breast Cancer
3-Day logo. Most Avon
3-Day material has been
removed from the Internet,
but this was taken from
a personal Web site
documenting one woman's
experiences in the walk.
http://jennifer.radiation.
net/avon3day.html.*

a situation that is particularly problematic in cities like San Francisco,
which in 2003 played host to a Race for the Cure, a Breast Cancer 3-Day,
and an Avon Walk for Breast Cancer, all in the space of three months.
And, while the organizing that Breast Cancer Action and its allies have
carried out around these issues has clearly been effective both in raising
public awareness and in prompting shifts in the practices of Avon, the
fact that the Komen Foundation was able to purchase the Breast Cancer
3-Day lock, stock, and barrel indicates the complexity of the struggle
they are waging. It is not simply a matter, as BCA is well aware, of rooting
out a few bad eggs. Rather, they are up against an entire system, firmly
embedded in capitalist consumer culture, and with enough resources to
continually adapt or respond to criticism by reinventing new strategies
through which to market their brands and hence to continue to define
the terrain on which the fight against breast cancer will be waged. While
the Think Before You Pink campaign discussed in chapter 1 is aimed at the
breast cancer marketing industry *in general* and therefore has the potential to address the corporatization of breast cancer activism at a systemic
level, the broader, and even more difficult, question of how to disrupt
the dominance of consumption-based expressions of political sentiment
and the displacement of more collective, more active, and more effective
strategies for social change remains stubbornly in place.

Chapter 3

Stamping Out
Breast Cancer

....

The Neoliberal State
and the Volunteer Citizen

So often when we read about breast cancer, we say,
"What can I do?" Now there's an answer: buy this stamp.
—Postmaster General William Henderson

Starting this week, all Americans will be able to open up
their hearts and mailboxes and help stamp out breast
cancer once and for all.
—Hillary Rodham Clinton

*T*he breast cancer research stamp, unveiled by First Lady Hillary
Clinton and Postmaster General William Henderson on July 29,
1998, costs forty-five cents and is valid for postage in the amount
of the prevailing first-class letter rate.[1] Seventy percent of funds raised are
donated to the National Cancer Institute (NCI) and 30 percent to the
Breast Cancer Research Program of the Department of Defense (DOD).[2]
This is the first stamp in the history of the United States to be endowed
with the capacity to raise funds for any institution or body other than the
U.S. Postal Service. In June 2004, the breast cancer stamp surpassed sales
of the Elvis Presley stamp to become the best-selling stamp of all time. By
June 2005, revenues from the stamp had reached $45.6 million, and by
November of that year, the NCI had collected $33.5 million, and the DOD,
$13 million.[3]

Following the ratification of the Stamp Out Breast Cancer Act (the legislation that brought the stamp into being), the 106th Congress witnessed
the introduction of fourteen more bills that would create fund-raising postage stamps, including the Alcohol Abuse Prevention and Treatment Trust
Fund Act, the Faces of AIDS Stamp Act, the Hunger Relief Stamp Act,

the Look Listen and Live Stamp Act (for rail grade crossing safety education), Organ and Tissue Donation Awareness "Semipostal" Stamp, the Stamp Out Diabetes Act, the Stamp Out Domestic Violence Act, and the Stamp Out Prostate Cancer Act.[4] In response, Congress signed into law the Semipostal Authorization Act on July 28, 2000, which authorized the postal authorities to sell special stamps promoting health, education, or any national interest without first seeking permission from Congress.[5] It was not until four years later, however, that a second "semipostal" was actually approved. On June 7, 2002, the Heroes of 2001 stamp, depicting

The Breast Cancer Research stamp.

Thomas E. Franklin's now famous photograph of three firefighters raising the U.S. flag at the World Trade Center site in New York City, was issued to generate funds for the families of relief personnel killed or disabled in the terrorist attacks of September 11, 2001.

That the second fund-raising stamp in United States history should emerge after September 11, 2001, makes sense in the context of dominant responses to the events of that day. While the Bush administration made plans for a military reaction, "ordinary" Americans were told that they could best help the nation to recover from this tragedy by doing two things: shopping and volunteering, with the donation of money a frequently cited example of the types of volunteerism in which people could engage. In his November 8, 2001, address to the nation, President Bush declared:

> Flags are flying everywhere—on houses, in store windows, on cars and lapels. Financial donations to the victims' families have reached more than a billion dollars. Countless Americans gave blood in the aftermath of the attacks. New Yorkers opened their homes to evacuated neighbors. We are waiting patiently in long security lines. Children across America have organized lemonade and cookie sales for children in Afghanistan.
>
> And we can do more. Since September the 11th, many Americans, especially young Americans, are rethinking their career choices. They're being drawn to careers of service, as police or firemen, emergency health workers, teachers, counselors, or in the military. And this is good for America.
>
> Many ask, what can I do to help in our fight? The answer is simple. All of us can become a September the 11th volunteer by making a commitment to service in our own communities.[6]

In this context, the Heroes of 2001 stamp offered an accessible and efficient vehicle through which citizens could fulfill both expectations at once: like so many recently created cogs in the machinery of philanthropic production in the United States, the stamp enabled people to do good for others at the same time that they went about their everyday practices of consumption.

As we have already seen, breast cancer nonprofit organizations, in partnership with corporate marketing executives, have led the way in developing consumer-oriented philanthropic activities over the past two decades. But during this period politicians at both the state and federal levels have also participated in the cultivation of breast cancer as a popular cause. Engaging in what a 1996 *New York Times* article called the "battle for the breast," politicians from across the political spectrum have responded to intensified organizing around the disease by offering highly publicized support for breast cancer initiatives, particularly those with a philanthropic component.[7]

Members of Congress became particularly interested in breast cancer, Carol Weisman argues, during the height of the abortion wars in the 1990s. The disease was viewed as a politically "safe" subject, "a good women's issue for both antiabortion and abortion rights legislators," that could help male legislators, in particular, win the allegiance of that most valuable, and slippery, of voters: the suburban, middle-class woman.[8] Weisman cites the case of Senator Arlen Specter, a mostly prochoice, fiscally conservative Republican who had famously and aggressively interrogated Anita Hill during the Clarence Thomas confirmation hearings and as a result found himself in trouble with women voters. In the face of his Democrat opponent Lynn Yeakel's renowned television campaign drawing attention to his behavior at the hearings and in an attempt to win back those voters, Specter became a key advocate of breast cancer initiatives in the 1992 election.

Mary Vavrus draws our attention to another key element of the historical context that helps explain political interest in the disease.[9] Her research reveals how the so-called gender gap in voting was by this period of time the primary metaphor employed to discuss women's electoral behavior (even though it was already known to be an unreliable tool by which to explain or predict voting choices). This pattern of voting, in which a significant percentage of women opt for one candidate and a significant percentage of men for the opposition, has been generative of a range of strategies designed to attract the votes of white, middle-class, suburban women who, accurately or not, were characterized by pollsters, politicians, and media pundits as swing voters. Vavrus also suggests that between 1992 and 1996 a key shift occurred in news discourse on women and electoral politics: in 1992 (The Year of the Woman), women were widely portrayed as wielders of political power, but in 1996 they came to be viewed as a demographic group of swing voters who were collectively designated as "soccer moms" and thus defined primarily by their filial obligations. Accompanying this shift, Vavrus notes, was an intensified ideology of consumerism in which electoral choices were increasingly reduced to "personal choices around product consumption and 'lifestyle.'"[10] In this context, it is not surprising that since the 1992 elections, numerous politicians—particularly those known for their conservative, antichoice, antifeminist (or some combination thereof) positions—made breast cancer a central part of their platform. And, moreover, that *consumption-oriented* philanthropy in the form of the breast cancer stamp became a primary tool for eliciting electoral support. In the 1996 elections, for example, conservative senators such as Rick Santorum of Pennsylvania, Jon Kyl of Arizona, Ted Stevens of Alaska, and John Warner of Virginia all vied for the "breast vote."[11] Another conservative Republican, Senator Lauch Faircloth, used his support of the breast cancer stamp during his reelection bid in 1998. In commercials that appeared on Lifetime television, Faircloth claimed, "For most people, a stamp is a way to send a letter. For one man, it's a way to provide hope." Faircloth strategists told the *Weekly Standard,* "We're trying to show people, especially women, that Lauch Faircloth is not an unreasonable guy. It did a lot of good for us. Tons. It's been one of the most successful spots in the campaign."[12]

Breast cancer also became a key issue in the race for the 2000 Republican presidential nomination. When George W. Bush made television commercials featuring Republican Party activist and breast cancer survivor Geri Ravish criticizing the record of Bush's Republican primary opponent, John McCain, on financing breast cancer "issues," McCain responded with publicity countering Ravish's claims and highlighting Bush's own failures to support spending on certain breast cancer programs.[13] Setting aside for a moment the question of the types of breast cancer policy that these politicians advocate (it is useful to point out that none of the men mentioned above scored highly by the National Breast Cancer Coalition's legislative criteria during that period), the enthusiasm with which conservative representatives now turn to particular forms of breast cancer activism might be suggestive of the sociopolitical norms and values that the disease has come to represent at this time.[14]

Indeed, in the process of tracing the history of political interest in breast cancer and, more specifically, the story of the breast cancer fund-raising stamp, it becomes clear how support for the battle against the disease is frequently generated through appeals that link success in this undertaking to the preservation of national motherhood, normative femininity, and the spirit of "American generosity," even as politicians of all stripes repeatedly attest to the bipartisan and apolitical "nature" of the cause. Moreover, although the breast cancer research stamp is in part a response to well-executed political organizing and an effect of the mainstream parties' efforts to attract women voters, it can also be understood as a symptom of the renewed political interest in volunteerism and philanthropy as modes of governing. In the context of the near blanket consensus that the era of "big government" is and should be at an end and of the concomitant cutbacks in state-funded social programs (but not, crucially in other realms), initiatives based on individual or corporate giving have come to be understood in dominant discourse as a more desirable alternative.[15] They are commonly viewed as more flexible, efficient, and personal than state-funded support, and participation in such activities is thought to build self-reliant, virtuous citizens. The promise of tools such as the breast cancer stamp is thus understood to go beyond the reduction of state spending to include a capacity for producing desirable citizens and new visions of U.S. society.

In his analysis of the history of neoliberal political thought, *Powers of Freedom: Reframing Political Thought,* Nikolas Rose has identified the desire to "govern at a distance" as a central tenet of mainstream politics in the United States and Britain in the past quarter century.[16] Neoliberalism has not abandoned the "will to govern," he argues, but instead reflects the pervasive view that the failure of government to achieve its objectives in particular realms is to be overcome by inventing new strategies of governance that will succeed. Frequently, these new strategies do not depend on the creation of more or better funded state programs and socially identified citizens who understand themselves as members of a single, integrated, national society; rather, they rely on the development of an enabling state that is no longer required to answer all of society's problems but that encourages and facilitates the active involvement of individuals, corporations, foundations, charities, schools, hospitals, community associations, and so on in resolving these problems. In this context, the story of the Stamp Out Breast Cancer Act, a measure that has enabled individual citizens to voluntarily participate in funding breast cancer research, provides a lens through which to explore contemporary political thought on the relative merits of state versus individual responsibility in providing for the common good and on the implication of the recent history of breast cancer in these debates.

The War on Cancer and the Debate about "Big Government"

It seems important to acknowledge here that discussions about funding for breast cancer research, screening, and education do not map neatly onto debates about "big government" or balanced budgets. Since the launch of the War on Cancer under the Nixon administration in 1971, a vast majority of politicians from across the political spectrum have consistently supported high levels of state spending on cancer research.[17] Moreover, such spending has generally found favor with the public. In both political and popular discourse, cancer research has been viewed as relatively uncontroversial, and spending increases are justified, often implicitly, through the assumption that large sums of money allocated to such research must eventually, by the "logic of tidal waves," simply overwhelm the disease.[18] In explicit justifications for big spending, advocates have frequently appealed to patriotism and the belief that the United States must lead the way in the fight against cancer. Thus, in the 1970s, the War on Cancer was made analogous at various moments to the fight against Communism, to smashing the atom, and to putting a man on the moon.[19] In the words of one observer at the time, to oppose big spending against cancer was to oppose "Mom, apple pie, and the flag."[20] More recently, the stakes involved in the battle against the disease have been made equivalent to those involved in high-tech warfare—Operation Desert Storm, for instance—and in the fight to preserve America's nuclear families.[21]

Although the consensus in favor of big spending against cancer has remained remarkably strong over the past thirty years, under current political conditions, almost any initiative that involves federal expenditures must address the now equally strong consensus *against* "big government" (recent exceptions would be the massive increases in military spending under George W. Bush). Thus, federal policy on breast cancer that requires increased public spending must be couched in the language of "government for good" (Hillary Clinton's words in an interview with the *Washington Post*) in order to disarticulate it from that which is understood to be "wasteful."[22] At the same time, initiatives such as the breast cancer research stamp, which are designed to incite personal generosity in the public, are justified and celebrated for their recognition that voluntary, philanthropic approaches to problems are inherently preferable to those that require state intervention, management, or financing.

The Politics of "Silly Objects" and "Substantive Politics"

It is equally important to address potential concerns regarding the intellectual value of engaging with a seemingly banal and trivial object—a postage stamp—at the expense of what might be viewed as more "vital" and "serious" aspects of federal breast cancer policy. An analysis of the breast cancer stamp, however, reveals much of note to say about the politics of breast cancer, gender, consumption, philanthropy, and the state. That is, in its absolute ordinariness, the stamp requires, to borrow Lauren Berlant's

words, an "intensified critical engagement with what had been merely un-
dramatically explicit." As Berlant has further argued:

> One does not find the materials of the patriotic public sphere theorizing
> citizenship in either beautiful or coherent ways. These materials frequently
> use the silliest, most banal and erratic logic imaginable to describe important
> things, like what constitutes intimate relations, political personhood, and
> national life.[23]

But what about the relationship of the breast cancer research stamp to
breast cancer policy more broadly? As I noted in the introduction, the past
two decades in the United States have witnessed the emergence of a multifaceted movement dedicated to fighting breast cancer. Made up of breast
cancer support groups, grassroots collectives, charities, national lobbying
organizations, corporations, and federal agencies, each with their own set
of priorities and principles, this movement has succeeded in placing breast
cancer at the forefront of both federal health policy and public interest
in matters of health. Unprecedented amounts of federal funds have been
directed toward breast cancer research. A slew of legislation designed to
regulate the quality of breast cancer screening, treatment, and care and
to increase the access of greater numbers of women to these services has
been enacted. Moreover, breast cancer survivors, like AIDS activists before them, have demanded and won involvement in the procedures through
which funds are allocated to research and through which clinical trials are
proposed, reviewed, and conducted.

As previously noted, scholars of the breast cancer movement have not focused their attention on what the National Breast Cancer Coalition (NBCC)
calls "pink ribbon proposals" and "awareness legislation," and for under-
standable reasons. Such proposals and legislation make up a substantial component of breast cancer policy, however, and frequently receive much more
mass media attention than what is known among activists as "substantive"
legislation.[24] The breast cancer stamp—which was not supported by the
NBCC in part because the organization feared that the creation of a "gim-
micky" stamp would mean a cutback in appropriations for breast cancer—
continues to receive extensive media attention and has been the subject of
several highly publicized unveiling ceremonies.[25] Post offices around the
nation have staged rallies and celebrations to advertise the stamp, often
with politicians and breast cancer awareness advocates in attendance.[26]
Numerous pleas for Americans to buy the stamp, several in the form of
mass distributed chain letters, have circulated on hundreds of electronic

mailing lists and Internet newsgroups. Senator Diane Feinstein has made her work on the legislation a central component of publicity drives.[27] And the Republican Party made the stamp the subject of a weekly radio address. In other words, legislation designed to incite and reflect the benevolence of the government and its citizens occupies a prominent site in public discourse on the fight against the disease. For this reason, a focus on the breast cancer stamp is not simply "white noise" that interferes with the more "serious" and "transformative" functions of activism and policy, as the NBCC rightly asserts, but as "powerful language" with troubling, material effects.[28]

The Passage of the Stamp Out Breast Cancer Act; or, The Generous State of America

Mass media stories attribute the idea for a breast cancer research stamp to Dr. Ernie Bodai, an oncology surgeon from California who had grown "frustrated by seeing woman after woman in need of a mastectomy."[29] After performing three mastectomies on one particular day, so the story goes, Bodai called Betsy Mullen, founder and CEO of Women's Information Network against Breast Cancer and "an indefatigable breast cancer survivor," and said, "We have to do something."[30] Bodai's idea for a stamp as the particular fund-raising vehicle they would use was apparently inspired when he looked at the stamp affixed to a National Institutes of Health newsletter that had arrived in the mail.[31] Although the idea of a stamp makes sense in terms of its communicative potential—stamps have long been used to circulate and commemorate national ideals—the justifications most frequently mentioned in the Bodai story relate to the fact that stamps are commonly purchased necessities and therefore easy and inexpensive vehicles through which people can participate in civic life.

A 1998 editorial promoting the stamp by Senator Diane Feinstein in the *San Francisco Chronicle* describes their ensuing efforts as follows:

> After brushing up on the legislative process with a high school civics book, these two marched up and down the halls of Congress to lobby on behalf of the stamp. They wore out shoes and spent thousands of dollars of their own money in support of their dream.[32]

References to the civics book and the personal dedication of Bodai and Mullen were made repeatedly in media coverage of the stamp.[33] Their successful lobbying was mobilized as evidence of the receptiveness of the state to hardworking, entrepreneurial citizens: "The stamp," Feinstein argued, "clearly demonstrates how ingenuity and hard work really can make a difference in how government works."[34] Moreover, Bodai's biography—he fled Budapest, Hungary, with his parents during the abortive anti-Soviet uprising of 1956 and spent a year and a half in refugee camps before entering the United States—helped reinforce the idea that the creation of the stamp was a reflection of the superior workings of American democracy: "I've learned government can be very responsive," Bodai told the *Los Angeles Times*.[35]

The passage of the act entailed minimal debate or opposition in Congress. Indeed, the House of Representatives approved the bill by a vote of 422 to 3 and the Senate by a vote of 83 to 17, making it one of the few votes in U.S. history to receive 100 percent voting in the Senate.[36] What little dissent there was focused on the possibility that administering the breast cancer stamp program would distract the "Postal Service from its responsibility of providing the best delivery service at the lowest price."[37]

The postal service did in fact initially oppose the act, fearing the precedent a fund-raising stamp would set and doubting that the public would be willing to pay to support it, but they relented "when they discovered how strongly lawmakers supported the concept."[38] Stamp collectors also opposed the bill, claiming that the surcharge on the stamp would be, in effect, a tax on their hobby.[39] "It's a wonderful idea," John Hotchner, president of the American Philatelic Society, told the *San Francisco Chronicle*, "but there are literally thousands of wonderful ideas. . . . The people who will end up paying are the stamp collectors of the world." However, even the lobbying force of Hotchner's 56,000 stamp collectors, who are responsible for $100 million in annual profits to the postal service, were, the *San Francisco Chronicle* claimed, "no match for Bodai."[40] Finally, resistance to the stamp circulated on the Internet among men who saw this as another instance of "gender bias" in the U.S. Congress. The "dads-rights" news group and the "dadlobby" mailing list, for instance, were the site of fierce opposition to the bill in 1997. In 1999, when a bill to create a prostate cancer research stamp was introduced into Congress, James Hayes, then Legislative Education Committee chair for the Fathers' Rights Association and director of the Men's Action Network PAC, declared this a "victory for men, the women who love them and their families."[41]

Some media outlets made note of the pockets of resistance in the postal service and among philatelists. And three editorials, in the *Boston Globe* and the *Buffalo News*, questioned the legislation. Ellen Leopold, the author of a book on the history of breast cancer surgery in the United States, criticized the decision to channel funds from the stamp to research rather than to treatment or follow-up care, claiming that this policy represented a long-standing bias in America's approach to fighting cancer.[42] The other editorials argued that the creation of the stamp signaled a dangerous turn away from general tax collections toward voluntary revenue enhancers and, by implication, toward funding priorities based on fashion rather than "worth."[43] Apart from these notable exceptions, however, popular discourse offered an overwhelmingly positive appraisal of the stamp.

Discussions of the bill in Congress were similarly enthusiastic, invoking a passionate consensus that ratification was the "right thing to do," particularly because it signified increasingly rare cooperation in the national legislature. Senator Feinstein called the ratification of the act the result of "a true bipartisan effort."[44] With reference to his Democratic colleagues with whom he had worked to introduce the legislation, Republican Representative John McHugh told the House, "I think it very clearly emphasizes the bipartisan nature of this bill and certainly recognizes the bipartisan tragedy that this disease can bring, and I urge all my colleagues to support this initiative." In a similar vein, Democratic Representative Sheila Jackson-Lee said, "Let me say that this is the best of the U.S. Congress. This act today, this exhibition of unity is really what this Congress is all about. Let me say that this stamp to help us stamp out breast cancer is the right way to go."[45]

As members of Congress waxed eloquent about the stamp's unifying potential, they also presented more specific arguments about the types of good work the stamp would do. They claimed it was an effective way to enlist grassroots participation in the fight against breast cancer and a means by which to inject consumption with ethical value and meaning, it was an ideal vehicle through which the state could enable the public to demonstrate their spirit of volunteerism and generosity, and it was a vital tool in the preservation of the nation's mothers and, by extension, nuclear families.

Grassroots Consumption

In pointing to the promise of the stamp for enlisting "grassroots participation" (a term increasingly used to describe individual consumption-based acts of philanthropy) in the fight against cancer, speakers deployed the mix of optimism, caution, and fear that so often characterizes discourse on cancer. In calling for the House to pass the bill, Representative McHugh pointed to the value of the stamp in terms of what it could contribute to the laboratory fight against "this deadly disease" and for the hope it would offer women:

> I know this proposal represents a necessary, thoughtful, and ultimately productive way to assist the Nation's scientific community in the vitally important quest for a cure of this deadly disease. . . . Today, through the adoption of this bill, the House has its opportunity to make a stand against this disease, and in the process, give every woman and including those who know, love and care for them, new hope.[46]

In a similar vein, Democratic Representative Vic Fazio said:

> We have made tremendous progress in raising money, in raising awareness, and in raising the spirits of so many in the battle against a disease that has devastated the lives of millions of loved ones, but we all know we still have a long way to go. I know that we will get there through the support of legislators in Congress and the grassroots support throughout our communities.[47]

And Representative Sheila Jackson Lee drew on the trope of the "small but powerful" to win the support of her colleagues: "I urge my colleagues to vote in favor of H.R. 1585, because if this option to give to the effort to end this unfortunate crisis saves one life, it has done more than enough."[48]

The passing of the act was also said to open up new ethical and political possibilities for the buying of a stamp, for what was previously conceived as a straightforward act of consumption. In this vein, Democratic Senator Barbara Boxer enthusiastically declared, "I am very excited about it. I can't wait to go to the post office and buy that stamp. If all the American people just think about buying a few of those stamps during the year, we will be able to put so much more into research. It is just a great concept."[49] Similarly, at the White House unveiling ceremony, Postmaster General William Henderson declared, "People purchase stamps every day, and now they can turn that simple act into a meaningful and effective way to participate in the fight against breast cancer."[50] And in a speech indicative of how both philanthropy via consumption and the fight against breast cancer are imagined in terms of middle-class lifestyle patterns, Republican Representative Susan Molinari told the House:

> I envision if we do this right an opportunity for people when it comes time for Christmas shopping, when it comes time for birthday presents, alongside with the little gift, you buy them a roll of stamps so that individual knows that

you might have spent an extra $5 or $10 to give your friend a present that also went toward reducing the risk of dying from breast cancer in this country, I also believe that it will take us a little less pain when we pay our bills if we know that while we are paying those bills, sending off those credit card company payments that we may also be contributing to finding a cure for cancer. Husbands, daughters, brothers and sisters will all have an opportunity to buy a stamp toward saving a life. I, like so many other women and men, would appreciate knowing that I helped make a difference in the fight against breast cancer just by spending a few extra pennies for a stamp I needed anyway.[51]

The Enabling State and the Active Citizen

The assumption that quick, convenient, and relatively inexpensive acts of giving have nonetheless powerful effects and deep spiritual meaning constitutes a common theme in contemporary discourse on philanthropy. The significance attributed to such acts stems in large part from their association with ideals of active citizenship, or from the notion that citizenship in the contemporary moment should be less about the exercising of rights and the fulfillment of obligations and more about fulfilling one's political responsibilities through socially sanctioned consumption and responsible choice.[52] In this new configuration, the government is seen to be at its best when playing the role of the facilitating state; that is, the state that *enables* Americans to pursue self-fulfillment through acts of generosity, if they so choose. In Representative Molinari's words: "I believe the American people will rise to the challenge of saying if we make it easy for you, if we make it an opportunity in your daily life of completing chores to donate to breast cancer, they will all absolutely rise to that challenge and help us conquer this disease."[53]

The figure of the ideal citizen as consumer is thus closely connected to the figure of the citizen as volunteer. Indeed, strategies of government designed to replace the passive, dependent citizen of the welfare state with the active consumer-citizen of neoliberalism have frequently placed, often with great public fanfare, volunteer-development programs at their core. It is in this context that we can make sense of the emphasis placed by politicians on the opportunity the stamp offered for Americans to *voluntarily* fund an important cause. Articulating the stamp to Bill Clinton's then recent call for a renewal of America's philanthropic culture (the President's Summit on Volunteerism had been held in Philadelphia three months previously), Representative Fazio told the House:

H.R. 1585 remains true to the idea of the American public participating in the search for a cure for breast cancer. By passing H.R.1585, we will be enabling the people of the United States to demonstrate a spirit of volunteerism to advance our successes in finding a cure for breast cancer. I think the ball is passed to those people who have made it so important that this Congress consider this legislation. They will be able to prove the degree to which their voluntary spirit and community commitment can produce the results we all seek.[54]

Speaker after speaker drew on the same theme: "The legislation is entirely voluntary," said Democratic Representative Tom Lantos. "That is one of the beauties of this bill. It is a completely voluntary method of raising money for a worthwhile cause," said Representative Molinari. "For the first time in our Nation's history," she continued, "the Stamp Out Breast Cancer Act will give Americans, every American, the opportunity to become more personally involved in funding breast cancer research."[55] In a similar vein, Senator Faircloth claimed, "When breast cancer strikes a wife, a mother, a sister, or daughter, it deeply affects the whole family. That's why I believe finding a cure for breast cancer is a fight worth making. A new postage stamp is a simple, voluntary way for all Americans to participate in that fight against breast cancer."[56]

Thus, the creation of the breast cancer research stamp was viewed as a way of democratizing philanthropy, of giving "all Americans" the opportunity to participate in what is popularly understood as a self-actualizing and socially productive practice. Moreover, in contrast to mandatory taxes, which are widely held to quash the civic impulses of Americans and to alienate citizens both from one another and the government, voluntary leverages are seen to elicit civic participation and personalize the relationship between citizens and the state. Thus, at the same time that this discourse of "access" and "opportunity" works to displace questions about the ability of *all* citizens to partake equally in these new forms of civic action, tools such as the breast cancer stamp also serve to legitimate the dispersed and privatized state and strategies of government-facilitated volunteerism and philanthropy.

In turn, media stories to demonstrate that individual Americans responded to the stamp as its creators had hoped abounded. An article that appeared in the *Arizona Republic* was typical in its focus on the meaning and value of the breast cancer stamp to a "featured" survivor:

Lynn Benjamin rarely gave a thought to the stamps she bought. Flowers? Birds? Love? Does it really matter? These days however, only the goddess Diana graces her envelopes, a choice that costs Benjamin only 8 cents extra per stamp. As a breast cancer survivor, the Coral Springs, Fla., woman knows the values of the breast-cancer research stamp.[57]

Calling the "manifold value" of the stamp "incalculable," Lynn Benjamin told the *Republic*, "The stamp may remind women to get a mammogram, to be aware of their bodies. It also will provide funding for research to find a cure for this devastating disease, and it will give hope to women with breast cancer by showing them things are being done."[58] Benjamin's claims about the pedagogical potential of the stamp characterized much popular and political discourse on its launch and were reinforced by the fact that post offices all over the country have offered breast cancer education (in the form of stressing the importance of early detection) and on-site mammography during special promotions of the stamp.[59]

Breast Cancer, AIDS, and National Motherhood

Congressional discussions about the stamp, which was unveiled by Senator Faircloth in Chapel Hill and by Senator Feinstein in Los Angeles to coincide with Mother's Day, frequently justified its creation by pointing to the threat the disease posed to women's roles as reproducers and nurturers of the American family. Representative Lantos, for instance, claimed, "More than 1.8 million women in America have been diagnosed with breast cancer, and an additional million more are unaware that they have breast cancer. It affects our wives, our sisters, our mothers, our daughters, all American women." Similarly, Republican Representative Constance Morella said, "I rise in support of H.R. 1585, the Stamp Out Breast Cancer Act. It enhances the quality of life, it enhances and keeps families together."[60] Although Representative Jackson Lee made reference to "women who are nurturers," she was also the only congressperson to acknowledge women in their capacity as breadwinners, a position that is consistent with her reputation as one of the few members of congress who brings health and other issues that disproportionately affect women, particularly poor women of color, into public discussions:

> It is a disease that can be in the body of women over a period of time without their knowing it: young women, women with children, women with promise, women with a future in front of them, women who are dynamic and yes, day-to-day women who are nurturers and workers every day keeping this country going.[61]

The threat that breast cancer poses to women in their capacity as nurturers—and with it the apparent inability of dominant culture to think about breast cancer as a disease affecting anyone other than the implied middle-class, heterosexual woman whose primary identification is as a mother or wife—is a regular theme in broader discourse on the disease. During his 1996 reelection campaign, Bill Clinton specifically connected his support for the fight against breast cancer to the importance of family values. In a speech in Springfield, Virginia, he reminded his audience of his administration's record on breast cancer policy as he stood before a banner bearing the slogan "Strengthening America's Families." Noting his mother's death from the disease two years previously, he said: "Nothing is more devastating to a family's strength than when someone is diagnosed with a life-threatening disease like cancer. I know about this from my own family experience, and nearly every family does."[62]

A similar theme characterized Hillary Rodham Clinton's breast cancer advocacy work. In May 1995, she introduced the "Mama-gram," an insert for Mother's Day cards and flowers that urges women to schedule mammograms. The "Mama-gram" was the result of a partnership between the federal government and the private sector (FTD Florist's Network and American Greetings) and was celebrated, like the stamp, as an example of the worth of public-private partnerships in the fight against breast cancer. The *Washington Post* went so far as to suggest that Rodham Clinton's involvement in the White House breast cancer campaign was likely to succeed, in a way that her participation in efforts to enact health care reform had not, because of the "compelling, personal tone" of the issue:

> His [Bill Clinton's] wife has emerged with a moral authority that was missing in the health care reform debate. On this subject she presides as an empathetic advocate: coaxing older women into action, enlisting children and grand-children as supporters, even recruiting men to join the effort.[63]

Robert's analysis exemplifies the transformation of Rodham Clinton's image during her husband's term in office from masculine, domineering, and independent feminist to good mother, sympathetic wife, and compassionate volunteer. It also demonstrates how, in public culture, breast cancer is articulated to gender norms that link normative femininity to the moral guardianship of the personal and the private, while the "serious" business of health care reform, demonized as it was through the discourse of "big government," is disarticulated from such norms.

The effectiveness of breast cancer activism, then, is understood to stem not from well-executed political organizing, but from empathy among politicians for the impact of the disease on "innocent"—read properly domesticated, feminine, and middle-class—women. For example, in her explanation of the success of the National Breast Cancer Coalition, Susan Ferraro of the *New York Times Magazine,* wrote:

> As the coalition's clout has grown, the powerful scientific and legislative communities that perhaps inevitably resist change have begun to hedge their objections to the advocates' assertions and demands. It's hard if not impossible to criticize mothers and sisters who are fighting cancer.[64]

In constructing breast cancer as, above all else, a threat to women in their capacity as wives and mothers and hence to the ability of the middle class to reproduce itself, discourse on the appeal of breast cancer often draws contrasts, both implicit and explicit, with popular constructions of HIV/AIDS. In one example, Amy Langer, then executive director of the National Alliance of Breast Cancer Organizations (NABCO), told *Working Woman* magazine, "Because AIDS was so public and so on the margin, breast cancer was by comparison relatively easy to square with corporate values."[65] The threat to the heteronormative nuclear family is of course a major trope in discourse on AIDS, but in the case of AIDS this threat has from the beginning been personified in the bodies of those demonized groups through whom HIV was first made visible—gay men, sex workers, IV drug users, and poor people of color. With breast cancer, however, the danger is imagined to come not from a particular group of people but from the disease itself, albeit in ways that remain replete with a range of cultural meanings. John Davidson of *Working Woman* draws this distinction in stark terms:

> Unlike AIDS, breast cancer can't be attributed to questionable behavior. Breasts may be a sexual part of the anatomy, but they are also symbolic of motherhood and nurturing. Moreover, the 180,000 women struck by breast cancer each year and the women who surround them—mothers, daughters, sisters, friends—represent a large and important group of consumers.[66]

While, contrary to Davidson's claim, risk and blame for breast cancer *are* commonly located in individual behaviors and "choices"—diet, exercise, age at childbearing, and especially commitment to regular mammograms—these behaviors are not directly associated with racialized, deviant sexuality or illegal drug use. The inference in Davidson's words is that among people with breast cancer there are, thankfully, no men, no gays or lesbians, no IV drug users, and no sex workers. So although discourse on breast cancer, like discourse on AIDS, often works to blame the victim and thus to deflect attention from structural or external variables that are implicated in incidence rates, the degree of demonization and pathologization of those with breast cancer is radically different. Indeed, what is most disturbing about the frequent comparisons between organizing around AIDS and organizing around breast cancer is the way that these narratives ultimately work to celebrate women with breast cancer at the expense of people with AIDS.[67]

Although these quotes on "AIDS versus breast cancer" derive mainly from breast-cancer-related marketers, in a social context in which marketing and electioneering and consumption and citizenship are so closely intertwined it becomes difficult to disentangle the history of political interest in breast cancer from the history of corporate interest in the disease.[68] So while business executives might be more explicit than elected officials about the political and economic "uses" of breast cancer, the battle for the breast vote, the constant refrain about the bipartisan "nature" of the issue, and the harnessing of the disease to rhetoric about family values are all part of a process in which politicians have joined with marketers in the co-construction of breast cancer as "an apple pie issue" that now comes with "built in assurance . . . that it's noncontroversial."[69]

The Politics of Breast Cancer

Dominant discourse to the contrary, breast cancer, like any other disease, is always already controversial. For evidence of a lack of congressional consensus on breast cancer, even among those who claim otherwise, one has only to peruse the NBCC's 1999 voting record to see that just one out of five of their legislative priorities for the First Session of the 106th Congress—a $175 million appropriation for the Department of Defense Peer-Reviewed Breast Cancer Research Program—were met.[70] When support for the fight against breast cancer takes the form of providing Medicaid coverage for the treatment of low-income women diagnosed with breast and cervical cancer, or providing coverage for the routine patient care costs of Medicare beneficiaries who are participating in clinical trials, or enacting a comprehensive and enforceable Patients' Bill of Rights, or passing a law to prohibit public health insurance and employment discrimination based on genetic information, many fewer congresspersons demonstrate their support. In this light, any claims about the uncontroversial nature of breast cancer as a political issue must be seriously questioned.[71] In other words, the creation of the stamp and the passing of the appropriations bill can be understood within the context of a well-established history of bipartisan congressional support for big spending on cancer research and within a more recent context of America's affective investment in breast cancer "awareness."

But the significance of the political struggle bound up with the creation of the breast cancer stamp exceeds the realm of electoral politics. The Stamp Out Breast Cancer Act was able to garner such solid support in Congress in part because its passage relied, to a large extent, on the assumption that no one can be *against* voluntarily raised funding for breast cancer research. In this context, any critical thought or debate about the stamp would appear misguided and mean-spirited. To oppose the bill would be to position oneself against voluntary fund-raising for a good cause and against finding a cure for breast cancer. To support the bill, on the other hand was framed as common sense: a demonstration of benevolence, of genuine investment in the search to find a cure, and of the belief that voluntary, private fund-raising for social causes is inherently preferable to the corrupt, coercive, and partisan mechanisms of state funding.

Thus, as this discourse constituted the breast cancer stamp as "uncontroversial" and "above politics," it simultaneously made it difficult, if not impossible, to speak against it or to question this mode of approaching the fight against the disease. The remarkable level of assent garnered by the breast cancer fund-raising stamp might be viewed, in other words, as testament to the political valence of increased funding for breast cancer research regardless of the precise orientation of investigation, to how difficult it is to think or speak critically of philanthropy and volunteerism at this moment in history, to the reduction of civic life to family life, and to the hegemony of an ideal of public life based on the sentimental desire to "make a difference" through individual acts of consumption. The stamp became, in other words, a mechanism for limiting how people think about, speak of, act upon, and constitute the disease.

Chapter 4

Imperial Charity

Women's Health, Cause-Related Marketing, and Global Capitalism

> *The Avon Foundation is a grassroots phenomenon, saving lives one person, one step, one dollar at a time, and we express our deepest gratitude to all those who make it possible—private citizens, Avon Sale Representatives and employees, and corporate supporters.*
> —Katherine Walas, *Avon Foundation News*

*H*aving successfully captured U.S. public interest in breast cancer, nonprofit organizations, pharmaceutical companies, and other corporations have recently begun to pursue breast-cancer-related activities overseas. The Komen Foundation, the most aggressive pursuer of corporate relations and consumer supporters among the large breast cancer organizations in the United States, established its first international chapters in Germany, Greece, and Italy in 2000. Their inaugural Race for the Cure event outside the United States was held in Rome that same year. In 2004, AstraZeneca, the maker of tamoxifen and numerous other cancer drugs and the creator of Breast Cancer Awareness Month (BCAM), launched Redefining Hope and Beauty, which they describe as the "first global breast cancer awareness campaign." Although the company's claims about the "global" reach of the effort are somewhat exaggerated (at the time of the launch, Redefining Hope and Beauty was supported by eleven charities in ten countries), there is no doubt that they have the resources to "reach previously inaccessible audiences across the globe and expose them to BCAM's traditional messages."[1] And while AstraZeneca was careful to minimize its ownership of the campaign in press releases and other forms of publicity, this language does little to conceal the company's desire to open up new markets for its products through messages of "awareness" and "early detection."

Describing itself as the "leading corporate supporter in the battle against

Avon advertises its international philanthropic programming, Avon Walk for Breast Cancer, Boston, May 16, 2004. Photograph by the author.

breast cancer," the Avon corporation runs the most extensive "global" breast cancer program, with more than fifty countries participating in its endeavors in 2004.[2] Avon has been a major force in the world of breast-cancer-related marketing within the United States since 1993.[3] A year before, the company began to orient its overseas fund-raising activities to women's health issues when it launched the Worldwide Fund for Women's Health. Over the course of the next decade Avon gradually adopted an almost exclusive focus on breast cancer and helped lay the groundwork, if unintentionally, for the kind of project now undertaken by AstraZeneca.

The entry of corporations and nonprofit organizations into transnational philanthropic endeavors raises a number of important questions related to corporate giving, women's health, and global capitalism. Here I focus on three in particular: the social commitments that are enabled and constrained when "economic freedom" is pursued through the language and structures of global corporate philanthropy, the use of breast cancer as the specific vehicle through which corporate interests are advanced, and how such philanthropic endeavors might help shape the social history of the disease on a "global" scale.[4]

In considering the first question, it is helpful to think about the now familiar observation that political, economic, and technological changes over the past two decades have removed barriers from markets that until recently were closed or highly regulated. Although the specific effects of the end of the Cold War, the emergence of international trade blocs, the expanding influence of bodies such as the World Trade Organization, and the availability of new technologies are the subject of ongoing debate, it is generally acknowledged that corporations play a more central role in international relations of power than they did prior to this period. Among scholars and activists of the left, there is a consensus that these shifts have produced a massive upward redistribution of monetary and other resources and an increased burden of poverty and debt on the world's poorest nations.

The economic and legal trajectories of the current global order have emerged in coincidence with a profusion of local, regional, and transnational nongovernmental organizations (NGOs) and social movements that constitute in the eyes of some commentators a burgeoning global civil society. The extraordinary diversity of NGOs and social movements in existence, however, in conjunction with the multiple, often contradictory, meanings of civil society in circulation, make coherent theoretical analyses of this phenomenon decidedly difficult. Fredric Jameson's discussion of the two distinct levels at which the idea of civil society operates is useful in this respect. He points out that this term signifies both the political "freedom" of social groups to negotiate their political contract and the economic "freedom" of the marketplace as a dynamic space of innovation and production, distribution, and consumption. Crucially, however, he notes that there is frequent slippage between the political and the economic as one level is "slyly" substituted for the other in "a kind of ideological prestidigitation."[5]

Here I am concerned with analyzing one particular site of such symbolic conjuring: the emergence of global corporate philanthropy and community relations (GCPCR) programs focused on breast cancer. In contrast to the mostly random, eclectic, and unscientific approach to corporate giving that dominated until recently, GCPCR programs, like the "domestic" corporate philanthropy discussed in chapter 1, take a highly measured, profit-conscious approach to this activity. Businesses often explain their move to create GCPCR programs in terms of both a need to "fill the breach" caused by a widespread reduction in the number and depth of government-provided welfare and health care services worldwide and heightened public concern and expectations about corporate responsibility (although such explanations are usually couched in language that suggests that corporations themselves have played no part in the downsizing process).[6]

In addition, GCPCR programs are one of a range of strategies by which transnational corporations seek to engage with "the local" in order to demonstrate that they enjoy more than a commercial connection to the multiple sites in which they conduct business and to recognize the differences (cultural, social, and so on) among them. While claims about "filling the breach" are not merely rhetorical maneuvers—the rise of antiglobalization movements over the past decade is evidence of heightened public concern as a reality faced by corporations—the history presented here posits economic and managerial imperatives, as much as ethical considerations, as the spur to their creation. Moreover, while the specific content of GCPCR programs is sometimes generated locally and therefore varies across national borders, the analysis that follows suggests that these programs are often cursory efforts that are more effective in building a coherent and readily identifiable "global" brand image than they are in tackling the specific issues they purport to address. In other words, as corporations seek to produce and sell goods in an ever-expanding number of locations, philanthropy and community relations are increasingly deployed not merely to further some social good, but as techniques for market penetration and retention, both in the domestic market and abroad.

The "Globalization" of Corporate Philanthropy and Community Relations

Despite frequent references to the growth of GCPCR practices among U.S. corporations in literature on corporate social responsibility, there is a paucity of empirical research on the global or transnational dimensions of strategic community relations. In the literature that does exist, the claim most often made is that GCPCR programs have become an important part of many companies' public relations strategies as corporate operations are increasingly globalized.[7] Given its infancy relative to domestic community relations programming, however, as well as management and accounting complexities (in terms of whether a cash contribution, for instance, originates from local business operations outside or within the United States), GCPCR is difficult to measure.

There is, nevertheless, some limited information available. Anne Klepper of the Conference Board found that corporate executives most often cite improved personal and government relations, enhanced corporate image, and a boost in market penetration as the major advantages of global contributions programs.[8] In other words, GCPCR is seen by businesspeople to function as a strategic tool for multinational corporations. The Conference Board has also recorded the contributions of U.S. corporations to non-U.S. beneficiaries since 1983, and it is possible to discern from these figures that the increasing internationalization of corporate operations has been accompanied by greater giving overseas, although the figures do not show if giving is greater relative to pretax profits. Thus, Audris Tillman found that the median contribution of U.S. corporations to non-U.S. beneficiaries in 1983 was approximately $100,000, a figure that by 1988 had risen to approximately $175,000. By 1993, this number had reached $600,000, and although the median contribution declined to a low of $350,000 in 1996, it had climbed back to $700,000 by 1998.[9] Another Conference Board report found that 42 percent of surveyed companies currently have an international giving program and 10 percent intend to implement a program in the next three years; managers ranked North America, Europe, and Asia as the top three recipient regions.[10] A visit to the Web site of any global corporation confirms these figures and the importance corporations place on their GCPCR programs, with page upon page of images and text documenting their commitments made available to the online public. The Avon corporation is no exception: the company's U.S. Web site currently offers multipage, multilink descriptions of numerous programs, including the Avon Breast Cancer Crusade. In addition, several country-specific Avon Web sites, including those in Argentina, Australia, Dominican Republic, France, Malaysia, and South Africa, devote considerable space to describing the work their employees and representatives are undertaking in the struggle against the disease.

The History of Avon and the Politics of Gender

Founded in 1886 and recognized as a pioneer of door-to-door sales, Avon is currently the world's largest direct vendor of beauty products, with $6 billion in annual sales. The Fortune 500 company produces over 600 million sales brochures in more than twenty-five languages each year, and its products are sold to women in 143 countries through 3.5 million representatives. Despite its long history and sizable market, however, business analysts have expressed skepticism about Avon's ability to survive as a direct-selling organization that has relied for so long on the part-time labor and the custom of "housewives" in an era in which increasing numbers of women are in paid employment.[11] While sales in North America have been slow and sometimes stagnant over the past ten years (in 2003, sales in this region increased by 3 percent, while operating profits declined by 4 percent), profits garnered elsewhere have continued to grow steadily and commentators point to Avon's success in the Latin American and Asian markets, in particular, as the reason for their survival. Avon obtains two-thirds of its revenues from overseas transactions, and markets in Asia, Eastern Europe, and Latin America commonly post double-digit increases in sales and profits.

Thirty-one percent of its operating profit in 2003 came from Latin America alone, where the company commands 20 percent of the cosmetics market, four times its share in the United States.[12] According to Avon's 2003 annual report, the Russian market is "growing at extraordinary rates," with a 70 percent increase in sales in 2003. During the same year, sales in China rose by 20 percent to $157 million, prompting the company to write in its annual report that "China and its vast population remains our largest long-term opportunity."[13] As such, the Avon corporation is typical of the direct sales industry as a whole, which grew 269 percent between 1987 and 1997 and saw the number of salespeople increase by 336 percent during the same period, thanks in large part to increased business abroad.[14]

Avon entered overseas markets early on in its history, opening its first international office in Montreal in 1914. The company began selling in Venezuela in 1954, Japan in 1969, and China in 1990. In line with a more general move among corporations to present themselves as sensitive to cultural differences and, moreover, to present this sensitivity as somehow disconnected from profitability, Avon prides itself on its ability to adapt to local retailing cultures. In China, for instance, where door-to-door sales were made illegal in 1998, the company switched to distributing its products in what by 2006 totaled six thousand boutiques. In the Philippines, orders are not mailed but picked up at a central supermarket-style distribution facility, and in Japan most business is done via mail order.[15]

While Avon's sales and marketing techniques are designed to mesh with "local" cultures, under the direction of CEO Andrea Jung the company has moved away from regional toward worldwide branding. A multitude of local products have been replaced by "global brands" such as Avon Color (an extensive line of cosmetics), and the company launched its first international advertising campaign in 2000 at the cost of $100 million. Jung's vision for a new Avon is what she calls the "ultimate relationship marketer of products and services for women" and "the company that best understands and satisfies the products, service, and self-fulfillment needs of women globally."[16] While this move involves adding more products to the line, it also means that more attention is now paid to "ethical" relationships between brand, consumer, and salesperson through careful management, on a transnational scale, of the meanings and values that Avon employees and customers attach to the products they sell and buy.

Avon is thus part of a broader trend, in which brand management has moved from being little more than a corporate identity system, a logo and accompanying visuals built around the company name, "to something much broader, more professionally rewarding and, hopefully, more profitable for the company," according to Katherine Troy, director of the Center for Performance Excellence.[17] Brand management now seeks to ensure that the brand and the corporation's philosophy of responsible citizenship share the same "territory" in the minds of all those who interact with the company or the product (i.e., employees, subcontractors, government officials, and consumers). Under this approach, brand is seen as a "veritable covenant with the customer" and as a way to align the vision of the corporation with its employees, so that the brand is "leveraged internally and externally with equal force."[18] Avon has some success in its endeavors, according to *Business Week,* which in 2003 placed Avon on its "most valuable global brands list," awarding the company the highest rank of any cosmetics corporation.[19]

Avon's concern with cultivating a gender-progressive brand image is exemplified in the corporation's international slogan, "Avon: *The* company for women," and its move, in the face of constantly shifting gender norms and relations, to position itself as a prowoman corporation. Hence, repeated references in Avon's international advertising and public relations materials are made to the company's self-proclaimed radical beginnings:

> For more than a century Avon has provided women with economic opportunity and financial independence.

> Avon provided one of the first opportunities for American women to be financially independent at a time when their place was traditionally at home.

> Women have sold Avon since 1886—34 years before they won the right to vote![20]

Avon's prowomen image thus helps to mediate the disjuncture between contemporary sensibilities about appropriate gender roles—the blandness of the claims helps ensure that they articulate well with a diverse array of notions as to what these roles should be—and Avon's arguably dated image as a company of and for "housewives" who sell products devoted to the maintenance of "normal" femininity. The America-centric nature of these claims, moreover, suggests that Avon is exporting a vision of liberated American womanhood, in particular, under the guise of a universal femininity, in order to shore up their global brand image.

The Worldwide Fund for Women's Health and the Avon Breast Cancer Crusade

This process of mediation has also been enabled through Avon's entry into the realm of women's health. The Avon Worldwide Fund for Women's Health, launched in 1992, was a global initiative in which Avon operations around the world were encouraged to develop a women's health program. Through the fund, the stated mission of which was to "break the barriers— social, cultural, financial and medical"—to women's health, approximately $190 million was raised to support programs in thirty-four countries.[21] As the 1990s unfolded, the Avon Products Foundation, a United States–based 501(c)(3) charity, also began to present itself as an international actor, stating that its mission was to "improve the lives of women, globally," and that it aimed to become the "world's largest foundation for women."[22] Although most of the foundation's fund-raising and grant-making activities take place within the United States and the company does not reveal the exact nature of the relationship between the foundation and its overseas philanthropic activities, this language suggests that Avon began to make its charitable self-representation coalesce with its image as a global corporation during this period.

It is within this context that Avon undertook to recategorize and consolidate its transnational philanthropic programming by abandoning, in 2003, almost all references to the fund in its publicity materials.[23] Instead, Avon's U.S. Web site, where all press releases, reports, and other materials for public consumption related to its philanthropic initiatives are posted, now uses the heading "Global Impact" to direct readers to information about the numerous breast-cancer-related activities it conducts in countries around the world. In other words, Avon has transformed its focus on women's health issues in general into a focus on breast cancer in particular and has introduced new, snappier slogans—"Avon Breast Cancer Crusade" and "Kiss Goodbye to Breast Cancer"—through which to promote this new theme.

The types of programs found in thirty-one countries involved in the effort, the date they were established, and the causes they support are summarized in Table 1. There is some variation in the names assigned to the efforts, with Avon Breast Cancer Crusade and Kiss Goodbye to Breast Cancer the most common, but not at this point exclusive, choices. In locations such as Australia and the United Kingdom, Kiss Goodbye is a just one of a variety of campaigns run under the Breast Cancer Crusade umbrella, but in Indonesia, Malaysia, and the Philippines the overall effort is now known as Kiss Goodbye. Prior to this, Avon's philanthropic efforts in these countries were given much more generic, less catchy names—the Women's Cancer Program, Cancer Early Detection, and Women's Cancer Crusade, respectively—a change that suggests the increasing attention the company is paying to the promotional aspects of these efforts.[24]

The strategies through which funds ($300 million net in fifty countries worldwide from 1992 to 2003, according to company publicity) are raised for Avon's programs are also becoming more standardized, although there is still some variation across national locations. Physical-activity-based events, for example, appear to be increasingly popular fund-raising tools. In addition to the Avon Walk for Breast Cancer in the United States, there are walks in the Czech Republic, Hungary, and Japan. Moreover, some of the races in the Avon Running Global Women's Circuit, a transnational series of 5 and 10K competitive runs for women, have some community service component, even though this is not the primary purpose of these events. The 2003 Global Championship race, held in Bangkok in November, for instance, benefited the National Cancer Institute of Thailand, and at the Avon Running event held in Germany in the same year (according to publicity materials, the largest women's running event in German history, with 10,500 women from forty-four countries), information on breast cancer was distributed to 180,000 spectators.

Cause-related marketing is also a primary tool in Avon's repertoire. Various pieces of jewelry in the shape of a pink ribbon are among the most popular products marketed through this approach. In South Africa, gold-tone and silver-tone pink ribbon pins are sold for ten rand each. In Dominican Republic, silver crosses and pens with breast cancer insignia

Table 1. Avon's women's health programs

Region/country	Program title	Established	Cause
ASIA PACIFIC			
Australia	Breast Cancer Crusade; Kiss Goodbye to Breast Cancer added 2002	1996	Australia New Zealand Breast Cancer Trials Group; YWCA Encore Program (community support, through exercise and counseling, to women who have had breast surgery); $5 million (Australian) raised
Indonesia	Women's Cancer Program, now Kiss Goodbye to Breast Cancer	1995	Indonesia Cancer Foundation; early detection programs
China			Avon China donated 2 million renminbi of Avon "health-related products" to the China Charity Federation in its work against SARS
Japan	Avon Group Support; Walk for Breast Cancer	1983	women's organizations; breast cancer
Malaysia	Kesan Barah Awal (KEBAL) Cancer Early Detection, now Kiss Goodbye to Breast Cancer	1994	donation of Mammotome breast biopsy machine to Putrajaya Hospital; provision of screenings for "women in need"
New Zealand	The Gift of Life Breast Cancer Awareness Program	1996	breast cancer

Philippines	Bigay Alam ay Bigay Buhay (Imparting Knowledge is Giving Life); Women's Cancer Crusade, now Kiss Goodbye to Breast Cancer	1994	opened Breast Care Center at Philippine General Hospital with mammography machine donated by Avon Foundation
Taiwan	Foundation of Breast Cancer Prevention and Treatment	1999	breast cancer
Thailand	Women Running Against Breast Cancer; Avon Sue Rak . . . Pitak Suang (The Gift of Love from Avon . . . To Protect Your Breasts)	1998	breast cancer
EUROPE			
Czech Republic	Kampan proti nadorovemu Ochoreniu prsnika; Project Hope; Campaign against Breast Cancer	1998	The Alliance of Czech Breast Cancer Associations, Project Hope, the Helpline, and the Women for Women project
	Avon Walk for Breast Cancer	2003	breast cancer
Germany	Aktion: Bewußtstein für Brustkrebs (Action Awareness for Breast Cancer)	1999	breast cancer
	Mercure Day '96	1996	muscular dystrophy
	Avon Running event	2003	breast cancer

Region/country	Program title	Established	Cause
Hungary	Multidiszciplinaris csoportok as eml rak ellen (Multidisciplinary Teams Against Breast Cancer)	1998	cancer research, purchase of mammography machine
Ireland	Avon One-Day Walk for Life	2003	breast cancer
	Avon ARC Crusade Against Breast Cancer, now Breast Cancer Crusade	1998	Aftercare Research Counseling Cancer Support Center in Dublin to help women suffering with breast cancer
Italy	Italian League Against Cancer	1997	women's cancer
Poland	Wielka Kampania Aycia – Avon Kontra Rak Piersi (The Great Campaign for Life – Avon Against Breast Cancer)	1998	breast cancer
	Charity concert "Let's Unite in Hope" in 2002	2002	breast cancer
Portugal	Avon Breast Cancer Crusade	1999	breast cancer
Spain	Una Llamada de Esperanza Contra el Cáncer (A Flame of Hope Against Cancer), now The Vision Group	1994	breast cancer
Slovak Republic	Ready OKEY Leto 2002 summer festival	2002	breast cancer
Turkey	Meme Kanseri lle Mucadele Programi (Breast Cancer Charity Program)	1995	breast cancer

Country		Year	
United Kingdom	The Avon United Kingdom Breast Cancer Crusade (with Kiss Goodbye to Breast Cancer and Fashion Targets Breast Cancer as subsidiary campaigns)	1992	Partners with U.K. Breakthrough Breast Cancer; donations to Toby Robbins Breast Cancer Research Centre; £10 million raised in total
SOUTH AMERICA			
Argentina	Un Lazo por la Vida (A Ribbon for Life)	1992	Breast cancer (The Avon Argentina Web site claims that a mobile mammography unit funded by Avon has provided 53,600 free mammograms while traveling more than 55,000 km around the country. http://www.fundacionavon.org.ar/famsite/fam_salud/fam_salud_fam_y_salud.htm
Brazil	Fashion Targets Breast Cancer; Running Against Breast Cancer; Breast Cancer Program	1995	Four nonprofit organizations providing breast cancer services to medically underserved women; mammography machines installed in buses that will travel to small cities to offer women clinical exams and mammograms
	Created the Avon Institute to "guide social investments in women's health and well-being and support activities in the area of corporate social responsibility"	2003	
Chile	Cruzada (Avon) Contra el Cáncer de Mama(s) (Avon Breast Cancer Crusade)	1997	breast cancer
Venezuela	Avon, Una Flor de Esperanza en la Lucha contra el Cáncer (Avon, A Flower of Hope in the Fight Against Cancer)	1994	breast cancer

Region/country	Program title	Established	Cause
CENTRAL AMERICA			
El Salvador	"Just for Women" run	2002	Avon Breast Cancer Crusade
Guatemala	"Just for Women" run	2001	Avon Breast Cancer Crusade
Honduras	"Just for Women" run	2003	Avon Breast Cancer Crusade
NORTH AMERICA			
Canada	Avon Canada Flame Crusade Against Breast Cancer, now Breast Cancer Crusade—Reason for Hope	1993	breast cancer; CDN $8 million raised
Puerto Rico	Avon Cruzada Contra el Cáncer (Avon Crusade Against Cancer)	1993	breast cancer
United States	Avon Breast Cancer Crusade	1993	breast cancer
Mexico	Cruzada Nacional Avon Contra el Cáncer en la Mujer (Avon National Crusade Against Breast Cancer)	1993	women's cancers

are on offer in addition to pins. In Canada, the standard breast-cancer-related products are supplemented by stuffed bears, umbrellas, cosmetics cases, and bookmarks. Unlike most cause marketing programs, however, in which the burden of donation falls on the corporation, or the consumer, depending on one's perspective, Avon's programs often raise money through sales representatives forgoing their commissions.

The labor of Avon's 3.9 million representatives, who according to the company "constitute the world's largest force of volunteer breast cancer educators," is also central to other aspects of Avon's community relations programming.[25] With every pink ribbon product they sell, the salespeople hand out information about the disease as well as materials describing the programs and services supported by the Breast Cancer Crusade. A more elaborate effort is Give Information, Give Life in the Philippines, in which Avon sales teams are trained to give basic information on cancer to their clients, to demonstrate breast self-exams, and to give referrals to community health centers and medical practitioners. Thus, in line with the philosophy of strategic philanthropy, this program constitutes sales representatives as grassroots health care workers at the same time that it helps solidify an intimate connection between the products they sell and the causes they promote.

There are a number of levels at which practices such as these can be assessed. Most basically, it could be argued that, like other breast-cancer-related marketing efforts, these campaigns raise money for a worthy cause (although, as I asserted in chapter 1, often the amounts raised pale in comparison to the company's advertising expenditures on these campaigns) and help elicit public awareness of breast cancer, however generally defined. But this position raises its own set of questions: What exactly does "awareness" mean in the context of breast cancer, and what is it that consumers are being asked to gain "awareness" of? When Avon campaigns do venture into specifics, awareness usually means preaching the benefits of early detection through mammograms. Although this approach might prompt women to discover if they already have breast cancer, this selective brand of awareness asks women to take personal responsibility for fending off the disease, while ignoring more difficult questions related to what might be done to stop it at its source or, for that matter, to treat it once those underserved women whom Avon claims to assist receive a positive diagnosis.

This issue becomes even more complex when posed in transnational and cross-cultural contexts. Prior to the spread of the Breast Cancer Crusade

beyond the United States and the United Kingdom and an intensified concern for synergy between brand identity and philanthropic activity, there
was at least some local variation in the kinds of women's health issues
Avon's international operations addressed; now, however, these operations
appear to have been asked to make their activities coincide with those that
have proved most popular in their countries of origin. Moreover, even if we
accept that breast cancer is a problem at one level or another the world over
and leave aside for the moment questions of varying priorities in women's
health issues across different locations, Avon has produced no evidence that
I am aware of, in any of the places in which it operates, to show that a
focus on early detection is the most effective way to proceed. Nor is there
evidence that the company worked with local women's health groups or
community organizations to determine what their priorities might be (a
criticism that, as I mention in chapter 2, has been made of Avon's philanthropic initiatives in the United States). In fact, a comparative analysis of
the programs run under the Avon Worldwide Fund for Women's Health
and the new breast cancer programs, based on Internet sources collected
over the past six years, suggests that Avon is now less likely to direct proceeds to existing charities and foundations in the countries in which it operates than it was previously.

Another critical concern relates to the ideological work that these campaigns do in terms of constituting breast cancer as a primary problem in
places where it might be far from the most pressing issue on the women's
health agenda. Andiye, a Ghanaian activist and speaker at the 2002 World
Conference on Breast Cancer, makes the argument this way: "The greatest
risk factor facing women living in third world poor countries [is] living in
third world countries," and "powerlessness to change the 'national inequalities' that force people to inhabit unsafe/unhealthy environments is the
leading cause of cancer today."[26] Even within countries such as the United
States, Canada, and the United Kingdom where breast cancer is a major
cause of death among women, questions have been raised by health activists and professionals about the attention given to breast cancer above heart
disease or other conditions that kill more women each year. The (faulty)
assumption that breast cancer is a disease of white, middle-class women
(an assumption enabled in no small way by the images circulated in breast-
cancer-related marketing campaigns), whereas heart and lung disease are
seen as self-inflicted outcomes of a working-class "lifestyle," is at least in
part responsible for the interest in breast cancer in the United States. In this

context, it is important to consider how a focus on breast cancer might be disproportional to the risk it poses and what this might mean in terms of how health professionals and women perceive their risk of other diseases. Indeed, various studies have shown that women overestimate their chances of getting breast cancer and underestimate their chances of getting heart disease or lung or colon cancer.[27]

While recognizing the dangers of making generalizations about women's health on a national, let alone international, scale, these same concerns are relevant to Avon's transnational philanthropic practices. It is well known that breast cancer rates are considerably higher in Western industrialized countries than they are in the rest of the world. To give a sense of these differences, Table 2 shows comparative rates for some of the countries in which Avon operates.

It is clear from the figures in the table that age-adjusted incidence rates are much lower in Latin America, Southeast Asia, and South Africa than they are in the United States, Canada, and the United Kingdom. In every country in this table for which data are available, heart disease is the number one killer of women. In Dominican Republic and South Africa, AIDS is the biggest killer of women and girls under forty. Uterine cancer is more common, although also more treatable, than breast cancer among women in Southeast Asia. Cervical cancer is one of the leading causes of

Table 2. International breast cancer rates

	Age-adjusted incidence rate (per 100,000)	Age-adjusted mortality rate	Total number of deaths per year
United Kingdom	135.5	24.3	13,303
United States	101.1	19.0	42,913
Canada	84.3	21.1	5,305
Australia	83.2	18.4	2,667
Argentina	73.9	21.8	5,362
Philippines	46.6	27.1	7,532
Brazil	46.0	14.1	11,283
Dominican Republic	36.1	11.5	378
South Africa	35.0	16.4	2,790
Japan	32.7	8.3	9,178
Malaysia	30.8	13.5	1,292
Thailand	16.6	6.3	1,980

Source: World Health Organization (www.who.int)

death among women across developing countries, with the highest rates in Central America and sub-Saharan Africa.

This is not to argue that breast cancer is not a health concern in these locations, or that there is no need for research funding or access to screening and treatment. What it does suggest, rather, is that Avon may be helping to contribute to a culture of breast cancer risk on an international scale, and hence assisting to build an expanded market for the breast cancer industry. The chart also reveals that the differences between countries are much smaller when mortality rates are taken into consideration. This is surely an indication, among other things, of the need for access to treatment for breast cancer and health care in general, issues that are not of course addressed by the disbursement of Avon funds or the rhetoric deployed in its campaigns.

The Many Guises of Neoliberalism

The story that I have told here highlights how the Avon corporation, like other businesses that are seeking to produce and sell goods in an ever-expanding number of locations, has increasingly deployed philanthropy not merely to further some social good, but as a technique for market penetration and retention. Avon's practices, however, must be understood not simply in the context of a shift in business culture, but also, and crucially, as part of a struggle over how and by whom socioeconomic management on a transnational scale should be undertaken. In other words, their philanthropic programming, focused as it is on developing consumer-oriented, private, and individual responses to breast cancer in locations across the globe, articulates neatly with other, more prominent, and at this stage powerful and pervasive, neoliberal projects. For instance, World Bank and International Monetary Fund structural adjustment programs require cutbacks in public sector services in countries of "The South" and the former Eastern bloc and their replacement with private sector alternatives. Although Avon is not participating in a direct way in the privatization of schools, power supplies, hospitals, and so on, their activities are helping to produce market identities, values, and practices in the realm of women's health and, moreover, are contributing to a more generalized movement toward the commercialization of every facet of people's lives. In a similar vein, the World Trade Organization and a slew of international trade agreements pave the way for corporations like Avon to extend their global reach and profitability through a variety of policies that seek to allow the unimpeded flow of capital and to dismantle public, noncommercial goods, services, and forms of sociality that have the potential to diminish profitability.

More generally, the kinds of subjects that Avon's programs envision and inspire have much in common with the ideal subject of neoliberalism. The women who sell and buy Avon's breast-cancer-related products and who participate in other fund-raising and educational programs are self-responsible and responsible to others in voluntary and private ways. They are self-educated and knowledgeable about threats to their health. They are consumerist, active, and entrepreneurial. (This is true particularly of the sales representatives, who, it could be argued, symbolize the quintessential neoliberal worker: because they depend on sales commissions, they have no guaranteed income. Under neoliberalism this form of precarious employment is now given a positive value, as the goal of permanent lifelong work for all no longer represents a dominant social ideal.) And they enact their duties as citizens in and through the ever-expanding marketplace, rather than the public sphere.

In showing how the Avon corporation's GCPCR programs are related to other components of the neoliberal undertaking, I hope to emphasize a point made in the introduction. Namely, that neoliberalism is not a unitary system, but instead, in Lisa Duggan's words, a "complex, contradictory cultural and political project created within specific institutions, with an agenda for reshaping the everyday life of contemporary global capitalism."[28] Among the most prominent manifestations of this project within the United States in the past quarter century has been a renewed emphasis on the social promise of volunteerism and philanthropy in the wake of the near blanket consensus that the era of welfare government should end. By every administration since the election of Ronald Reagan in 1980, the American people have been told that the state can no longer be relied upon to mitigate the social effects of capitalism and that America's spiritual and material prosperity depends upon the charitable works and voluntary financial commitments of individuals and corporations. Avon is just one, albeit significant, example of a number of multinational corporations now taking the American version of generosity onto the world stage by underwriting "nonprofit" ventures in the name of community renewal, grassroots participation, and a revitalized global civil society. Although global strategic community relations programs are just one, often relatively small, part of any transnational corporation's overall business strategy, the chorus of corporate discourse on volunteerism, philanthropy, civic participation, and citizenship is growing ever louder. As such it should be taken seriously in struggles over what a global civil society might look like and how individuals and groups, within and across national borders, might negotiate the relationship between economic and political freedom.

Chapter 5

The Culture of Survivorship and the Tyranny of Cheerfulness

It was very important for me, after my mastectomy, to develop and encourage my own internal sense of power. I needed to rally my energies in such a way as to image myself as a fighter resisting rather than as a passive victim suffering. At all times, it felt crucial to me that I make a conscious commitment to survival. It is physically impor-tant for me to be loving my life rather than to be mourning my breast. I believe it is this love of my life and my self, and the careful tending of that love which was done by women who love and support me, which has been largely responsible for my strong and healthy recovery from the effects of mastectomy. But a clear distinction must be made between this affirmation of self and the superficial farce of "looking on the bright side of things."

Like superficial spirituality, looking on the bright side of things is a euphemism used for obscuring certain realities of life, the open consideration of which might prove threatening or dangerous to the status quo.
—Audre Lorde, *The Cancer Journals*

If I had to do it over, would I want breast cancer? Absolutely. I'm not the same person I was, and I'm glad I'm not. Money doesn't matter anymore. I've met the most phenomenal people in my life through this. Your friends and family are what matter now.
—Cindy Cherry, *Harper's*

*I*n the context of a historical moment in which breast cancer is widely understood as an enriching experience of the sort described by Cindy Cherry, Audre Lorde's words, penned on March 30, 1979, and subsequently published in *The Cancer Journals,* seem startlingly prophetic.[1] For the narrative describing the experience of breast cancer that has come to dominate the popular imagination in the United States in the past decade concerns itself almost exclusively with the "bright side of things." In the tidal wave of self-help and inspirational breast cancer books that have been published during the past few years (at least forty in the United States between 2000 and 2004); in heroic appearances on *Oprah* and *Lifetime Television;* in special advertising features in the *New York Times Magazine;* in the profusion of Internet Web sites, chatrooms, and message boards dedicated to the disease; and in rousing speeches at fund-raising events and political rallies, breast cancer survivors describe how the disease has helped them salvage failing relationships, boost their self-confidence, establish new friendships, rethink their priorities, get in shape, and find true happiness. As Barbara Ehrenreich points out in her essay "Welcome to Cancerland," there is even a well-established lore among breast cancer professionals and survivors that "chemotherapy smoothes and tightens the skin, helps you lose weight," and, when your hair grows back, ensures that it will be "fuller, softer, easier to control, and perhaps a surprising new color."[2] Moreover, these stories circulate alongside mass-mediated images of survivors who are uniformly youthful (if not always young), ultrafeminine, slim, immaculately groomed, radiant with health, joyful, and seemingly at peace with the world.

In certain respects, then, Lorde's vision has been realized: breast cancer is rarely viewed now as a shameful or self-induced disease and is, as we have seen, most often portrayed as an enriching and affirming experience during which women with breast cancer are rarely categorized as "victims" or "patients." There is also considerable evidence to suggest that "depressed and socially isolated people are more prone to succumb to diseases, cancer included," and that those women who are in a position to take advantage of the cheerfulness and optimism of breast cancer culture are likely to find that it aids in their recovery.[3] But Lorde's warning that to look on the bright side of things is to obscure realities that might prove threatening to the dominant order is more relevant now than ever before.

While it is quite common for illness to function as a transformative experience on an individual basis, often in positive ways, the dominant discourse of breast cancer survivorship, as I argue throughout the book, leaves little room for alternative, less positive, understandings of the disease experience and its long-term effects, or, relatedly, of the political-economic context in which the fight against the disease is being waged. And while research on women's experiences with breast cancer suggests a wide range of psychological responses to the disease—in other words, the dominant image of breast cancer as the route to true happiness is not borne out by the research—the heterogeneity of these experiences does not easily penetrate dominant discourse on the disease and the approach of the cancer establishment to it. Indeed, as Ehrenreich vividly conveys, despondency, anger, or dissent are frequently understood as a kind of treason within this tyranny of cheerfulness. Personal narratives that are less positive than the majority, for instance, must begin with an apology, as when "Lucy," whose "long term prognosis is not good," starts her contribution on breastcancertalk.org by warning us that her story "is not the usual one, full of sweetness and hope, but true nevertheless." And when Ehrenreich herself posts a statement on the Komen Foundation's message board under the subject line "angry," in which she lists a series of complaints about her treatment experience, "recalcitrant" insurance companies, and environmental carcinogens, she receives a tide of rebukes criticizing her for her bad attitude and, in one case, advising her to seek help.[4]

In addition to alienating women who cannot or do not share this "positive embrace" of the disease, the result of this "relentless brightsiding," Ehrenreich argues, "is to transform breast cancer into a rite of passage—not an injustice or a tragedy to rail against, but a normal marker in the life cycle, like menopause or graying hair."[5] In this way her concerns about the depoliticizing effects of the normalization of the disease echo Lorde's concerns: "Let us seek 'joy' rather than real food and clean air and a saner future on a liveable earth!" Lorde wrote with irony, "As if happiness alone can protect us from the results of profit madness."[6]

In contrast to the majority of breast cancer narratives in circulation today, Lorde was able to argue for the need for self-affirmation among women with the disease and, at the same time, engage critically with a number of issues rarely mentioned in contemporary mainstream discourse that emerged as she integrated the crisis of breast cancer into her life: the invisibility and silence of women with the disease, prosthesis, amputation, the cancer-industrial complex, the relationship between cancer activism and antiracism, widespread heteronormativity, and her confrontation with mortality. Her purpose was to encourage women to interrogate and speak out about the meaning of cancer in their lives and to use their experiences to work for change: "For silence," she wrote, "has never brought us anything of worth."[7] In the passage that serves as the epigraph to this chapter, her specific concern was with the blame-the-victim mentality of the breast cancer establishment, exemplified by a doctor who had written a letter to a medical magazine declaring that no truly happy person ever gets cancer.

The historical conditions that once allowed a doctor to declare that the truly happy never get cancer have shifted such that we are now asked to think about breast cancer as a route to true happiness. Whereas Lorde was concerned, in 1980, with the prevailing idea that one must be in the "right psychological frame of mind at all times to *prevent* cancer" (emphasis added), the national mind-set is now such that one must be in the right psychological frame of mind to *survive* the disease.[8] In this new framework, Ehrenreich argues, there is a sense in which the triumphalism of survivorhood denigrates the dead and the dying, a sense in which breast cancer survivors are understood to have somehow fought harder than those who have died, and a sense in which they are braver, better people than those who have succumbed to the disease.

One individualizing narrative has thus been replaced by another. The new version of individual responsibility allows women to get sick but not to die and, in circulating the ideal model of survivorship, succeeds in selling an enormous range of goods to consumers, raising millions of dollars for large nonprofits, and garnering votes for politicians eager to find an issue that positions them as prowomen but not feminist. This model also helps to maintain support for high-stakes, early detection, and cure-oriented research to the virtual exclusion of other avenues of exploration. As Ehrenreich writes:

> In the overwhelmingly Darwinian culture that has grown up around breast cancer, martyrs count for little; it is the "survivors" who merit constant honor and acclaim. They, after all, offer living proof that expensive and painful treatments may in some cases actually work.[9]

While breast cancer survivors are celebrated for their courage and strength within this model, their success at survivorship is seen to depend on their submission to mainstream scientific knowledge and reliance on doctors and scientists to protect them from death. They—and the public at large—are told to obtain regular screenings, demand insurance coverage for mammograms, explore a range of treatment options, and talk to other survivors, but they are discouraged from questioning the underlying structures and guiding assumptions of the cancer-industrial complex. The culture of breast cancer survivorship does not, in other words, embrace patient-empowerment as a way to mobilize critical engagement with biomedical research, anger at governmental inaction, or resistance to social discrimination and inequality, even if its history is bound up with attempts to do just this.

Illness, Identity, and Activism

Earlier in the book, drawing on the work of other scholars, I mapped some of the key forces that helped shape the emergence of a breast cancer movement in the United States. Like all histories, however, the story I told was partial. Missing from the narrative was an attempt to draw connections between the development of activism around breast cancer and political mobilization around other diseases, an analysis that is central to a fuller understanding of the emergence of the breast cancer survivor as a category of identity and the political trajectory that organizing around it has taken.

I begin this part of the story in the post–World War II era, when traditionally hierarchical relations that defined interactions between medical researchers, doctors, and patients came under widespread scrutiny. In the 1950s, writes Paul Starr in *The Social Transformation of American Medicine,* medical science had "epitomized the post-war vision of progress without conflict."[10] But in the decades that followed, a variety of groups and interests emerged to challenge this model. Alongside the efforts of the women's health movement, leftists mounted a critique of the profit-driven medical-industrial complex that, they argued, worked to benefit large corporations and shareholders rather than patients; liberals and conservatives alike began to question the burgeoning costs of health care; and revelations of ethical abuses in clinical trials and other forms of medical experimentation led to campaigns for informed consent legislation.[11] From these forces emerged a greater skepticism of medical experts and a shift away from established notions of the "proper" medical patient as passive, unquestioning, and deferential.

It was the AIDS movement that took shape in the 1980s, however, that really revolutionized the possibilities for disease activism in the United States. Rather than acting as what Steven Epstein calls a "disease constituency," which primarily functions to pressure the government for more funding, the AIDS movement became an alternative basis for expertise. In contrast to other models by which they could have positioned themselves in relation to medical science, AIDS activists did not reject science or seek to show that science and truth were on their side, but rather staked "out some ground on the scientists' own terrain." In other words, they fought AIDS both from outside and within medical science. And as they questioned the uses, controls, content, and processes of scientific practice, they also claimed "to speak credibly as experts in their own right." As such, according to Epstein, it became the first social movement to actually undertake the transformation of "disease victims" into "activist-experts."[12]

The efforts of activists to be involved participants in AIDS research and policy were inextricably intertwined with their struggle to eschew the widely held understanding of people with AIDS as "victims" of disease. Activists rejected this label, arguing that it elicited fear and pity, suggested inevitable death, allowed "spectators" to distance themselves from those with the disease and thus remain passive, and connoted some character flaw or bad "lifestyle choice" that had invited the tragedy to befall them.[13] Moreover, as Max Navarre contended, the fear and hopelessness that stem from constant reminders that "you are helpless, there is no hope for you" easily led to despair.[14] The aim of Navarre and others was to enable people with AIDS to understand themselves, and for others in turn to understand them, not *as* the condition but as people *with* a condition. Self-empowerment, he and others believed, breeds hope, and "hope is one of the greatest healers."[15] On the basis of these beliefs, in 1983 the National Association for People with AIDS adopted the Denver principles, which declared that people with AIDS had the right and responsibility to determine their own experience with the syndrome. The opening declaration of the principles reads as follows: "We condemn attempts to label us as victims, which implies defeat, and we are only occasionally 'patients,' which implies passivity, helplessness, and dependence on the care of others. We are 'people with AIDS.'"[16]

The recognition that identity categories, the means through which people with disease are labeled and categorized, could significantly shape the course of a disease and society's response to it has had profound implications for the formation and strategies of health activist movements in the wake of the AIDS epidemic. Through processes of what social movement scholars call "social movement spillover"—when new movements grow from the foundations of existing movements and borrow from their strengths and strategies—the health activist groups that emerged in the 1980s and 1990s, while diverse in their agendas, shared a sense of the importance of disease identity categories that suggested live, active, and empowered individuals. Among cancer activists, this shift was evidenced by the gradual disappearance of the label "cancer victim" (and to a slightly less extent, "cancer patient") from public discourse and its replacement with "cancer survivor"—a shift that was also surely shaped by the feminist movement against sexual abuse and domestic violence, which had undertaken to challenge the image of the passive battered woman with the same linguistic modification during the same period.[17]

This shift was given institutional legitimacy and form in 1986, with the creation of the National Coalition for Cancer Survivorship. Their organization was the first, NCCS claims, to define an individual diagnosed with cancer as a survivor from "the moment of diagnosis and for the balance of life." Since that time, NCCS has been a leading force in advocating for "survivors' rights" by lobbying for increased funding for cancer research and access to quality cancer care and sponsoring educational publications and programming. The founding of the NCCS was followed by the formation of other cancer survivorship organizations (the American Cancer Society's Cancer Survivors Network, for example) and a move on the part of existing organizations to place survivorship at the center of their missions and at the heart of their public relations activities. While in some cases a professed interest in "survivorship" was just another term for commitment to research on prevention, treatment, and cure, in other cases, "survivorship" came to represent a new realm of scientific concern, a hitherto neglected phase of the experience of cancer. A 1998 *Dallas Morning News* article explained the development as follows: "As many as 10 million Americans call themselves cancer survivors. Yet until recently, their well-being has been largely unexplored by most doctors and medical researchers."[18] As a result, the cancer survivor became, or rather was constituted as, a subject of scientific investigation, and a number of leading cancer organizations instituted programs to encourage the study of the physical and mental well-being of people who had lived through the disease. In 1996, the National Cancer Institute created the Office of Cancer Survivorship to encourage the study of the "growing number of cancer veterans." In 1998, the American Cancer Society and the Komen Foundation followed their lead with the launch of similar efforts.[19]

This short history offers an indication of the extent to which the empowered patient—the activist-expert, the survivor—has become institutionalized and incorporated into the fabric of the cancer establishment. This is nowhere more clear than in the case of breast cancer. The movement remains extraordinarily diverse, with support groups, grassroots collectives, charities, national lobbying organizations, corporations, and federal agencies working both in alliance and independently to shape the course of the disease. And although breast cancer survivors, like AIDS activists before them, have demanded and won involvement in the procedures through which funds are allocated to research and through which clinical trials are proposed, reviewed, and conducted, breast cancer groups, like Breast Cancer Action, that embrace patient-empowerment as a way to mobilize critical engagement with biomedical research, anger at governmental inaction, and resistance to social discrimination remain a small minority, swimming against the tide of pink ribbon perkiness.

Manufacturing Consent: The Co-optation of a Social Movement

How can we explain the rather smooth incorporation of the breast cancer movement? And what, if anything, would such an analysis suggest about the potential for alternative configurations to emerge and succeed?

In his attempt to explain the success of AIDS treatment activism, Steven Epstein argues that its early participants were "equipped with a whole set of resources crucial for engagement in the struggle over social goods and social meanings": HIV emerged on the heels of successful political organizing on the part of the homophile and gay liberation movements so that by the time the AIDS epidemic was recognized in 1981, members of the activist community were already deeply immersed in projects that sought to link "tangible political goals to the elaboration and assertion of an affirmative group identity."[20] The movement was also able to capitalize on the skepticism toward medical authority that had developed with the struggle to demedicalize homosexuality, a position that was enforced by members of the women's health movement who brought their critiques of the medical profession to their AIDS organizing. Most significantly, Epstein notes, gay communities, particularly those in urban centers, boasted preexisting organizations that were dominated by white, middle-class men—artists, intellectuals, health professionals, lawyers, policy makers, city officials, and so on—with the political clout, fund-raising experience, and substantial cultural and economic capital necessary to bring about social change.

Likewise, many of the breast cancer movement's most important figures were already economic and political "insiders"—lawyers (e.g., Fran Visco, president of the National Breast Cancer Coalition), surgeons and researchers (e.g., Dr. Susan Love, founding member of NBCC), successful businesswomen (e.g., Amy Langer of the now defunct National Alliance of Breast Cancer Organizations), journalists (e.g., Rose Kushner), longtime political activists (e.g., Elenore Pred, founder of Breast Cancer Action), and lobbyists who understood the workings of the political and medical establishments. The materialization of the movement was also enabled by preexisting political affiliations, including women who had been active in feminist politics, AIDS organizing, lesbian rights, and breast cancer support groups, although, as Jennifer Myhre argues, these sources made up a much more loosely related political, social, and medical network than that from which the AIDS movement developed.[21]

One way these two movements differ quite dramatically, however, is in the strategies they have employed to achieve their political goals. While many breast cancer activists emphasize the significant influence of the AIDS movement on their own efforts, among them those who received direct mentorship from AIDS activists on strategies for gaining access to the biomedical research establishment, there is evidence to suggest that the large organizations in the mainstream of the movement deliberately distanced themselves from the tactics and demeanors of AIDS activism, or at least those strands of AIDS activism that favored angry and dramatic confrontations over more orderly and measured approaches.[22] Patricia Kaufert, for example, has argued that when the National Breast Cancer Coalition

> eschewed the more radical tactics of ACT UP, it is likely that the decision owed something to a shrewd sense that it was important to draw a distinction between themselves and the AIDS activists. The Coalition's influence lay in emphasizing the very "ordinariness" of their members, a microcosm of American womanhood, angry but neither threatening nor contentious.[23]

Thus, whereas AIDS activists mobilized their abject subjectivities by, for instance, throwing their (fake) blood during direct actions, groups such as the NBCC consciously worked to produce a normalized identity for the movement. Their aim—and they were successful in this—was to woo politicians, leaders in the world of biomedical research, and, in the case of some groups, corporate sponsors, while at the same time hoping to avoid threats to their credibility that might spring from gendered responses to large groups of women acting in emotional or confrontational ways.[24] So although breast cancer activism has been characterized by the occasional foray into theatrical and provocative protests, even the more radical reaches of the movement have not engaged in the consistent, dramatic, and confrontational direct action that characterized the work of groups such as ACT UP. And while it was precisely the oppositional approach of AIDS activists that helped push the syndrome onto the front pages of the nation's newspapers and bring patients into the research process, the more conciliatory style and normative self-presentation of breast cancer activists brought similar accomplishments, in *addition* to huge investments on the part of corporate America and an agenda that congealed around a range of very narrow issues.

The co-optation of the breast cancer movement can also be explained by the fact that it has not addressed itself to the broader inequalities and normalizing social relations that over time began to concern prominent branches of the AIDS movement. This is not to suggest that the AIDS movement was from its inception, or is *as a whole,* more progressive or without its own set of political blind spots or limitations. Indeed, as Lisa Duggan writes in her discussion of the relationship between "love and money" in progressive politics, "AIDS activism exhibited all the conflicts and contradictions of liberal vs. radical strategies, legalistic political reform vs. cultural transformation, local vs. national and global agendas. Its organizations and institutions were (and are) marked by racism, sexism, and North-American centered arrogance."[25] Cathy Cohen provides an in-depth illustration of this point in the *Boundaries of Blackness: AIDS and the Breakdown of Black Politics,* where she argues that the racial blindness and racism of white organizers in AIDS organizations played a role in the failure to recognize AIDS in African American communities in the early 1980s.[26] Although the focus of activists on the homophobic roots of political apathy in response to the emergence of the HIV epidemic meant that they engaged in deeply challenging critiques of heteronormativity and homophobia, this approach also resulted in the privileging of sexual oppression over class inequality and racism. In fact, like breast cancer, AIDS was assumed, early on at least, to be a "white" disease. And, although, like breast cancer, this stemmed in part from the types of bodies through which it was made visible and the normalizing assumptions that then shaped the way researchers, medical professionals, politicians, and the media approached the epidemic, it was also a product of the demographic profile of early AIDS activists and the forms of unconscious racism that have historically plagued predominantly white organizations.

Similarly, various studies of the breast cancer movement have identified the profile of the average breast cancer activist as white, middle-class, middle-aged, and well educated.[27] In this respect, contemporary organizing around breast cancer retains many of the characteristics of the breast cancer awareness campaigns that began in the 1930s and which have been devised and managed since that time by prominent and powerful social actors. The historically entrenched homogeneous demographic makeup of the movement goes some way to explaining the particular agenda it has embraced and the fact that issues relating to forms of oppression based on class, sexual identity, or race have been marginalized in favor of a careful and nonthreatening focus on women (not feminists) as a constituency and breast cancer as a single issue that is presented as a mainly scientific, rather than economic, environmental, or social problem.[28] The issues that came to define the mainstream of the breast cancer movement after the initial campaigns against one-step mastectomies—involvement in the research process, research funding, awareness, support—were thus easily appropriated as focal points by large commercial entities with an interest in developing a consumer base for their products. Indeed, one of the central arguments of the book has been that breast cancer became a philanthropic cause par excellence not simply because of effective political organizing at the grassroots level, but because of an informal alliance of large corporations (particularly pharmaceutical companies, mammography equipment manufacturers, and cosmetics producers), major cancer charities, the state, and the media that emerged at around the same time and was able to capitalize on growing public interest in the disease.

As I noted in the introduction to the book, scholars trying to understand the "success" of the breast cancer movement have frequently turned to social movement theory for an explanation.[29] Unlike most social movements studied by sociologists, which are categorized as "conflict movements" because they are typically supported by minorities or slim majorities of the population and are confronted with fundamental, organized opposition, the breast cancer movement has lacked a countermovement and thus enjoys widespread public, institutional, and financial support.[30] On these grounds, Jennifer Myhre argues that the "consensual" nature of the breast cancer movement aided rather than hampered its cause: since very few people are "against" breast cancer activism or "for" breast cancer, the movement has enjoyed broad popular and institutional backing. In this context, the argument goes, opposition to breast cancer funding or the inroads that activists have made into the arenas of scientific decision making look petty and coldhearted and lack the momentum to succeed.[31]

Such analyses are useful for assessing some of the factors that have enabled the mainstream breast cancer movement to succeed in fulfilling its goals, and they correlate well with the argument presented in chapter 3 about the bipartisan appeal of particular strands of breast cancer policy among politicians and the public at large. What these arguments tend to underestimate, however, is the extent to which the disease has been naturalized *as* uncontroversial by the dominant form of activism that has grown up around the disease, particularly insofar as this work has disarticulated breast cancer from broader issues, such as the fundamental inequality of the American health care system or environmental degradation. As we have seen, there exists among activists, researchers, medical professionals, and politicians quite diverse perspectives on what causes breast cancer; how it should be prevented, detected, and treated; and how the funds raised to combat the disease are best distributed. A quick perusal of the congressional voting records on breast cancer over the past fifteen years reveals that once the debate moves beyond "pink ribbon proposals" such as the breast cancer stamp, there is very little unanimity on the subject. It is important to recognize, therefore, the extent to which the disease has been *constructed* over the past two decades as a unifying issue that is somehow beyond the realm of politics, conflict, or power relations.

The erasure of points of conflict and sites of struggle in the realm of breast cancer is a consistent feature of media coverage of the disease. Breast cancer has been variously described as a "safe" concern, as an "apple pie" issue, as "blissfully without controversy," and as coming with a "built in assurance . . . that it's noncontroversial," in the words of Amy Langer.[32] Moreover, as described in chapter 3, breast cancer is frequently contrasted with AIDS, particularly in terms of their respective appeal to politicians seeking to win voters and corporations seeking to attract consumers.

In some respects, the bases for these comparisons make sense, even if the way they are couched ends up reinforcing normalizing assumptions in extremely problematic ways. Unlike AIDS, which initially became visible through the bodies of already marginalized and demonized social groups— gay men, injecting drug users, sex workers, and so on—breast cancer was made visible through such figures as Betty Ford, Shirley Temple Black, and Happy Rockefeller, icons of all-American, hypernormal femininity. And whereas AIDS came to be viewed in dominant discourse as a punishment for immoral behaviors and lifestyles, explicit blame-the-victim discourse in relation to breast cancer is almost nonexistent at the present moment, although prevailing ideas about how to prevent the disease are heavily bound up with notions of individual responsibility and "choice" in the realm of commitment to regular mammograms and so on. The fact that breast cancer affects a highly valued part of the human body that is both sexually charged (at least in Western cultures) and symbolic of a woman's role in reproducing life has also made it more conducive to a positive public response.

So while there is veracity both to the claim that the political and corporate reaction to breast cancer has been different from the reaction to HIV/AIDS and to the contention that this difference can be explained, in part, by the meanings about the conditions that were already in circulation, it is important to recognize that both sets of responses stem from social ideologies and not the inherent "nature" of these conditions. It is the social history of breast cancer and the meanings that have developed in association with it that have made the movement more ripe for incorporation than its equivalent in the fight against HIV/AIDS. There is nothing inevitable, in other words, about how breast cancer—or AIDS for that matter—is understood and responded to in the public domain. Indeed, as Marita Sturken reminds us in her discussion of "AIDS kitsch," HIV/AIDS has its own, albeit shorter-lived, smaller-scale, and less spectacular history of commercialization and incorporation.[33] Both conditions, moreover, have been subject to social stigma, although certainly the attitude to breast cancer prior to the 1970s was not as hysterical or as violent as the public response to AIDS in the 1980s.

The historically contingent character of popular perceptions of breast cancer becomes particularly clear if we look back to the early 1990s, when the breast cancer activism that was most visible in American culture was not subject to "competition" from corporate activism: in this period, the public focus was more oriented to thinking about breast cancer in relation to the broader neglect of women's health and the rights and needs of women as a group. This is not to say that all, or even most, of the women involved in breast cancer activism during this time saw their work as part of a feminist battle against systemic oppression, but rather that the concerns of the movement were more socially and structurally oriented. Regardless of political inclinations, that is, it was regarded as a *collective struggle*. The focus was not, as it is now, on the individual breast cancer patient and her participation in uplifting and profit-generating activities to fund high-stakes medical research to the virtual exclusion of other considerations.

The Personal and the Political

Through the course of researching and writing this book, my thoughts have frequently returned to Audre Lorde. Her *Cancer Journals* have been a major inspiration for this work, and I have often found myself wondering what she would make of the present state of affairs. For the public response to breast cancer in the present moment is dominated by precisely the kinds of misplaced optimism and hyperfaith in mainstream science and medicine that she warned against, even if the social discrimination and stigma toward women with breast cancer that so concerned her has dissipated somewhat. Beyond her critique of prevailing attitudes toward the disease, however, Lorde also offered a way of thinking about the relationship between the personal experience of illness and social change that recognized the importance of individual empowerment without viewing it as an end in itself. In other words, she emphasized what she called the "militant responsibility" of women to involve themselves actively in their health. She wrote of the need to fight despair and to live beyond fear by "living through it." And she strove to promote the "possibilities of self healing and the richness of living."[34] But she did so always with a view to making these personal struggles politically useful. As she wrote in the introduction to the *Cancer Journals:*

> I have found that battling despair does not mean closing my eyes to the enormity of the tasks of effecting change, nor ignoring the strength and the barbarity of the forces aligned against us. It means teaching, surviving, and fighting with the most important resource I have, myself, and taking joy in that battle. It means, for me, recognizing the enemy outside and the enemy within, and knowing that my work is part of a continuum of women's work, of reclaiming this earth and our power, and knowing that this work did not begin with my birth nor will it end with my death.[35]

Here Lorde illustrates the possibility of moving beyond the paradigm that frames women with cancer as either passive victims or heroic individuals. She does not dismiss pleasure and endurance as sources of empowerment and thereby reminds us, for instance, of the potency of the kinds of physically challenging activities that are so popular among women who want to play a part in the fight against the disease. But for Lorde, it was important to channel these personal sensations into political concerns and to use them to open rather than close her eyes to the broader social struggles of which the fight against breast cancer was just one part.

Of course, the women who participate in breast cancer survivor culture bring to it, and take from it, a variety of political interests and experiences.

During the course of my research, for example, I spoke to one woman who was a longtime feminist activist in the small university town where she lived and who also volunteered many hours with the local chapter of the explicitly nonfeminist Komen Foundation. In spite of her commitment to the organization, she expressed quite strong critiques of the group's ideological orientation and her desire to push its thinking on issues such as health care and the environment. I have also been told about, though was not able to interview, more than one person who took part in the Avon Walk for Breast Cancer and felt angered both by the "no expense spared" approach and the individualist ideology that characterized the event. These fund-raising activities, then, sometimes themselves provide the conditions of possibility for resistance. The problem, of course, is that breast cancer culture as currently configured does not encourage these kinds of critical responses—Komen Foundation founder Nancy Brinker told the *Philadelphia Inquirer* in 2004 that she has no time for activists' "whining and kvetching"—and is in fact structured to close, rather than open, the context in which participants understand the problem of breast cancer to exist.[36] Audre Lorde thought that it was possible—and vital—that people recognize "the deep and fundamental unhappiness with which we are surrounded, at the same time as we fight to keep from being submerged in it."[37] Perhaps one challenge for those who seek to transform breast cancer culture, then, is to work *against* submersion in happiness and *toward* recognition of the deep and fundamental problems that surround us, both within the realm of breast cancer and beyond.

Conclusion

Beyond Pink Ribbons

*A*lthough there is often an expectation that a critique such as the one presented in the preceding pages will be followed by an outline of a political program or a set of policy proposals, that has not been the aim of this particular book. Instead, I have sought to offer a genealogical account and critique of the place of organized giving under neoliberalism. In articulating and reiterating my position as to what is at stake—politically, economically, and socially—in the current preoccupation with consumer-oriented philanthropic practice, however, it does seem important to engage with what are, in my view, both the most promising and the most problematic characteristics of the present culture of breast cancer activism.[1]

Prevention, Detection, and Treatment

Turning first to shifts that relate specifically to breast cancer prevention, detection, and treatment, it is clear that the ubiquity of awareness campaigns has encouraged a heightened attentiveness about breast health among women with access to these promotions, a change illustrated by their increased overall utilization of mammography, for example. Their sense of risk, however, is now exaggerated relative to other illnesses, a situation that helps to keep the market for breast cancer products, from genetic testing to teddy bears, buoyant.[2]

At the same time that corporations such as Avon, alongside federal and state governments and the large foundations, have assisted in spreading the doctrine of early detection, they have also improved financial access to screening among the underserved (although their access is far from perfect) and the quality of mammography facilities. The limited focus of consumer-oriented activism, however, shaped as it is by an ideology of individualism and an imperative for uncomplicated, snappy marketing slogans, has allowed for the emergence of a preoccupation with early detection to the virtual exclusion of other approaches to fighting the epidemic (e.g., prevention) and a failure to address the barriers, financial and otherwise, to treatment. This has resulted in a situation in which uninsured women with breast cancer have more reliable access to screening but are frequently left with no means to receive treatment after diagnosis. Even if this particular inadequacy of the health care system in the United States were to be addressed in a systematic way by the breast cancer movement, research has shown that being uninsured is of less consequence than poverty (though clearly these two factors intersect) in explaining why economically disadvantaged women are more likely to be diagnosed with a later stage of breast cancer and to have higher mortality rates.[3]

As long as the breast cancer agenda is dominated by multinational corporations and their nonprofit partners, there is little hope that the "barriers and burdens" encountered by poor women will penetrate the peppy public consciousness or elicit the kinds of policy responses that might actually make a difference to them.[4] Indeed, one of the key features of the neoliberal state is its refusal to view the amelioration of poverty as one of its central obligations or to view the "subject of compassionate action," to quote Lauren Berlant, as "any member of a historically and structurally subordinated population."[5] In the current formation, those who are recognized as suffering legitimately and as deserving of the protection of the state are working citizens or women, epitomized by the dominant image of the breast cancer survivor, who stay at home to raise a family while their (male) partners earn their keep. In this context, the very appeal of breast cancer as a site for collective compassion and generosity has come to depend on its distance from any notion of structural inequality and, in its current configuration, contributes to the (re)production of the notion that suffering, be it physical, emotional, economic, or otherwise, is actually an opportunity for individual growth, empowerment, and achievement.

Research Funding and Structure

There is no doubt that since 1990 there has been an exponential increase in private and government financial investment in research, even if the money-making potential of many of the most prominent and popular fund-raising vehicles tend to be exaggerated, with a high percentage of monies going to marketing and administrative costs. Unfortunately, the effectiveness of the "tidal waves" approach to breast cancer science is yet to be proved, as significant changes in incidence and mortality rates have failed to material-ize. In spite of this reality, the amount of money flowing in to the breast cancer cause, alongside the prominence of a discourse of survivorship in the culture at large, has engendered an exaggerated optimism about the level of progress made in the fight against the disease. The words of a Breast Cancer Action (BCA) pamphlet make the extent of the hyperbole clear:

> The fact remains that women diagnosed with breast cancer today face essen-tially the same treatment options—surgery, radiation and chemotherapy—that were offered when the War on Cancer was first declared nearly thirty years ago. And when it comes to prevention, the only options we are given are powerful pills with dangerous side effects, and surgery more drastic than that often prescribed for women with the disease.[6]

The lack of coordination or regulation of money flooding in for the cause (thirty government agencies and a host of large nonprofits, corporations, and biotech and pharmaceutical companies are all involved in funding and/or conducting research) has produced an approach to research that is ut-terly fragmented, with both needless repetition and massive gaps. This is why groups such as BCA are suggesting a new approach to research that will be "outcome" rather than "hypothesis" driven and will be conducted in several large interdisciplinary research centers located across the country. Again, as BCA states:

> [Needed is] a coordinated, adequately funded approach to breast cancer research, with the ultimate goals of understanding the causes of breast cancer and the reasons for different incidence and mortality rates among different racial and ethnic groups, and discovering more effective, less toxic treatments. Outcome-driven research, in which the researchers look for answers to these types of questions of most concern to the affected community, is necessary to achieve our goals. As a new approach to the standard scientific model, outcome-driven research frames the hypothesis to get the answers we need to important public health questions.[7]

Approaches to Health Activism

While a new model of organizing breast cancer research is surely needed, it seems unlikely that the battle against the disease will be won so long as it is approached as a single-issue problem or, more specifically, as a single-issue problem that is unrelated to broader cultural, social, economic, and political forces. That is, the narrow focus of most breast cancer activism mitigates against significant change occurring across the continuum of disease incidence and mortality rates in general, as well as in the realm of breast cancer specifically. The concern here is not so much with whether or not increases in breast cancer research funding have come at the expense of spending on other diseases, but rather with how such a singular focus prevents activists, policy makers, the media, and the public at large from understanding questions of health and illness in the larger context from which they arise. Lisa Duggan makes a similar point in her discussion of the reproductive freedom and women's health movements. She explains how, in the 1960s and 1970s, a broad network of local organizations and mobilizations "focused on sterilization abuse as well as abortion rights, on broad-based women's health activism as well as on legal strategies, on sexual as well as reproductive freedom." During the 1980s and 1990s, however, "this field of social activism, and the critique of the medical establishment and drug industry's profit-making ploys as well as their patriarchal hierarchies and racist agendas, largely receded from public view." "Broad-based feminist health activism persisted," she writes, "but narrow, single-issue lobbying, litigation, and fund-raising organizations such as the National Abortion Rights League emerged to focus action and energy on the defense of Roe v. Wade."[8]

In a similar vein, although there are groups within the breast cancer movement who work in coalition with other organizations on broader issues, it is the narrow, single-issue liberal lobbying and fund-raising organizations that have come to dominate national politics and media coverage. In turn, questions related to the effects of social and economic structure—particularly the lack of socialized medicine and the impact of the environment—on disease incidence, treatment, and mortality have been pushed to the margins in favor of a focus on educating and inspiring individuals to take responsibility for their health. Unfortunately, this approach seems set to continue as other "disease constituencies" explicitly seek to model themselves on the breast cancer movement.

The prostate cancer movement is among the most prominent of these emerging networks, with a plethora of local and national organizations (e.g., the National Prostate Cancer Coalition, the American Prostate Society, the Prostate Cancer Action Network, US Too!) heightening "awareness," pressuring the federal government to increase spending on research, organizing cause-related marketing partnerships with a range of corporations, running physical-activity-based fund-raising events, and even campaigning for a fund-raising research stamp. The movement, moreover, is actively reinforcing the single-issue, competitive model of disease activism by creating organizations and slogans such as "US too!"; "Save the Males!"; and "Men Get Prostate Cancer, Women Don't: And if they did everyone would know about it." Despite the antifeminist, antiwomen, anti-breast-cancer-movement sentiments in which such language trades, prostate cancer groups do join together with lobbying powerhouses such as the Komen Foundation at strategic moments to pressure the government to serve their interests.[9] Perhaps what we are witnessing, then, is the emergence of a new generation of large, corporate-funded, single-issue health foundations and advocacy groups (the American Cancer Society, the American Lung Association, and the American Heart Association would in this scheme represent the older generation), which share in common a strategic use of consumer-oriented identity politics (divorced from redistributive or social justice aims) to enjoin their constituents to take care of their health and to lobby for greater funding for particular kinds of research and education. While they might work together behind closed doors at certain times, the public face of these organizations is singularly focused and their chosen diseases carefully disarticulated from questions of broader social discrimination or material inequality.

In this context, the work of more expansive health movements with wider agendas and radical perspectives becomes exceptionally pressing. AIDS activism, which, in spite of the limitations explored in chapter 5, offers a particularly promising model in this regard. Although AIDS activists remain focused on one particular illness, they have formed what is truly a transnational movement, within which, as Lisa Duggan writes, "radical critiques and broad visions of democracy and equality . . . have flourished around the world."[10] The range of issues they address include access to health care and medication, trade and intellectual property law, debt cancellation, poverty, housing, homelessness, racism, gender inequality, and education. Moreover, in working to address AIDS in this broad way, they collaborate frequently with other activists in what is commonly referred to as the "antiglobalization movement" and thus also contribute to a much broader project to oppose neoliberalism and promote alternative ways of organizing social life.

Emotional, Social, and Political Connections

One of the most remarkable changes to occur within the past quarter century of breast cancer history in the United States is the destigmatization of the disease (at least in the public sphere) and the increased visibility of women who are suffering from it. In addition, there are now many more opportunities for women with breast cancer to build emotional, social, and political connections with one another, often through participation in fun, fulfilling, and collective activities. During my research I met women who used the Race for the Cure as a space in which to first declare their experiences with the disease; I talked to others who were desperately scrabbling to find the last few dollars they needed to enter the Avon Walk for Breast Cancer to make a public statement about their love for family members who were suffering with the disease (while these instances highlighted for me how meaningful such events were to the participants, they also raised troubling questions about their exclusionary structure); and I heard from yet others who found great comfort in spotting another woman on the street wearing a breast cancer pin or set of earrings. These are legitimate and meaningful experiences that have become available to large numbers of women, albeit across a fairly narrow socioeconomic spectrum. Given the critiques I have offered of this model of approaching the disease, however, is there a way in which its negative consequences can be addressed in ways that won't erase or negate its more socially productive effects? The emergence of what I have called a "tyranny of cheerfulness" provides no place for those women who cannot or do not wish to view their condition as a lucky gift. But is it not possible to retain the publicness of the breast cancer experience and refuse to wear the disease as a badge of shame and at the same time to recognize the failings of the current approach to fighting the disease? The histories of social movements ranging from civil rights to anticolonial struggles to AIDS activism suggest that anger and pride are not mutually exclusive emotions and, in fact, can work quite productively together in bringing about social change.

Unfortunately, the fact that the culture that has grown up around breast cancer shores up the most problematic elements of hegemonic femininity helps mitigate against such developments. In her attempt to understand the popularity of stuffed bears and other commodities more commonly associated with childhood as gifts with a breast cancer theme, Ehrenreich wonders if in some versions of the prevailing gender ideology, "femininity is by its nature incompatible with full adulthood—a state of arrested development." "Certainly," she writes, "men diagnosed with prostate cancer do not receive gifts of Matchbox cars."[11] Breast cancer culture, in other words, depends on and reproduces the infantilization of women and their status as only partially developed citizens. Moreover, it is clear that the industry that has developed around breast cancer depends on the exploitation of women's responsibility for, and identification with, shopping, as well as their historically embedded role as unpaid charity workers whose labor helps mitigate the social effects of capitalism, even as their work and the system it supports remain largely invisible. In this context, a feminist perspective continues to be crucial to understanding and intervening in the corporate mobilization of neoliberal notions of active citizenship, volunteerism, and community in the interest of market penetration and retention.

Neoliberalism and Beyond?

As I have argued throughout the book, what we are confronting in the emergence of consumer-oriented breast cancer activism is not simply a shift in business culture and the response of activists to it, but rather a struggle over how and by whom socioeconomic management should be undertaken. In other words, while the particular struggle over what constitutes the problem of breast cancer and how it might best be responded to is profoundly significant *in itself*, the corporatization of breast cancer activism and the emergence of personal and institutional philanthropy as the most legitimate and prominent manifestations of citizen involvement in the fight against the disease are, at another level, just one set of *symptoms* of a much broader set of social, political, and economic conditions.

These conditions, as mapped in the preceding chapters, include the development and deployment of a whole range of programs and techniques designed to encourage donations of time and money among the American public. The acts of generosity that result are viewed not so much as ends in themselves, however, but, rather, as crucial steps toward rekindling the culture of generosity that is said to have been stifled by large government programs and toward producing citizens who are personally responsible, active, and benevolent to those who are deserving of such generosity. In this respect, the argument presented here suggests that the current cultural preoccupation with philanthropy is driven not so much by a desire to find alternative ways of funding projects for the public good, although this is certainly a concern, but rather by an aspiration among innumerable social actors and institutions representing ideologies that span the political spectrum, to find new modes of producing, shaping, and governing proper citizens. As tools such as cause-related marketing, mass participation fund-raising events, and state-sponsored voluntary revenue enhancers become increasingly common vehicles through which individuals participate in "public" life, they also contribute to the formation of an increasingly corporatized and privatized "public" sphere in which political sentiment is properly expressed by the purchase of products or the donation of money. Because these tools rely on and gain their legitimacy through the good intentions of citizens, moreover, they are particularly resistant to critique or dissent.

Of course, as I wrote in the introduction, it is hard to overestimate how difficult it is to speak critically about any form of philanthropic activity in the United States at the present time. The period since September 11, 2001, has seen an intensification of the normalizing discourses that tie philanthropic activities to proper citizenship. While the Bush administration has enacted a far-reaching and brutal military response, "ordinary" Americans have been told that they can best help the nation to recover from this tragedy by consuming and volunteering, and any activity that falls outside these narrow confines of acceptable citizenship, or which seeks to question its parameters, is deemed suspicious, if not outright dangerous. It seems particularly crucial, then, at this point in history, to find ways to make visible the relations of inequality, obligation, and exploitation that structure well-intentioned charitable practices. It is my hope that this book has made some small contribution toward that end.

Acknowledgments

*T*his project has been supported by grants and awards from the Department of Kinesiology, the Women's Studies Program, and the Graduate College at the University of Illinois, Urbana-Champaign; from the Physical Education Program and the College of Education at the University of Arizona; and from the School of Physical and Health Education and the Principal's Development Fund and Advisory Research Committee at Queen's University. Since it is hard to know how or where to begin to thank all those who have helped me along the way, I will start with the teachers and mentors who were responsible for introducing me to the intellectual thinking and political engagements that shaped this project: Charles Jenkins, Hart Cantelon, C. L. Cole, John Lie, Cameron McCarthy, and Paula Treichler. I am particularly grateful to Sonya Michel for her guidance during the early stages of this work.

I received excellent research assistance from Karen Daigle, Tiff Mochinsky, Megan Preston, Jennifer Scott, and Sarah Sproule. Zoe Hammer and Caren Zimmerman also worked with me on this project. I am grateful to Zoe for her friendship and for countless nights on the porch of the Pink Palace. In addition to being a dear friend, Caren is responsible for keeping my Pollyanna tendencies in check. Dereka Rushbrook has been an outstanding formal and informal research assistant, an unparalleled tour guide, and a good friend.

For their crucial feedback and extensive suggestions on earlier versions of this work, I am grateful to Barbara Brenner, Maren Klawiter, Lori Reed, and Geoff Smith. I am especially thankful to Mary McDonald for her detailed comments and general enthusiasm about the project.

I thank Radhika Mongia for her invaluable friendship and intellectual support and guidance. Mark Althouse, Amy Hribar, Lisa King, Craig Robertson, Marya Ryan, and Dan Vukovich made life among the cornfields academically stimulating and so much more fun than I could ever have imagined. I am also grateful for the theoretical and political education I obtained at the hands of my comrades in the Graduate Employees' Organization and the Foucault Reading Group.

I am indebted to my friends and colleagues in Tucson, where I spent three happy years during the writing of the book: Ari Anand, Paul Burkhardt, Pat Fairchild, Miranda Joseph, Elizabeth Lapovsky Kennedy, Erin Leahy, Spike Peterson, Gary Rhoades, Louise Roth, Sheila Slaughter, Sandy Soto, and Scott Watson. I especially want to thank Eliane Rubinstein-Avila for her love and support during the past six years.

The companionship and professional support of Mary Louise Adams made the transition from Arizona to Ontario much easier than it would otherwise have been. In no small part thanks to her, I now have a wonderful group of colleagues and friends: Chris Bongie, Elizabeth Christie, Stevenson Fergus, Dina Georgis, Helen Humphries, Susan Lord, Dorit Naaman, Daintry Norman, Kip Pegley, Elaine Power, Sarita Srivastava, and Janice Deakin—the best department head one could ask for.

I thank my friends back in England—Georgina Archer, Stephanie Bridgeman, Katy Davies, and Victoria Harper—for sustaining our relationship over such long distances and for such a great period of time. I am also grateful to Carole, Peter, Matthew, Shiva, and Alexia for the ongoing love and support that made this possible.

Finally, it has been a great pleasure working with Richard Morrison, my editor, whose enthusiasm for the project and vast knowledge of research in relevant fields have been invaluable.

Notes

Introduction

1. Lisa Belkin, "How Breast Cancer Became This Year's Hot Charity," *New York Times Magazine,* December 22, 1996, 40–46, 52, 55–56.

2. Susan Ferraro, "You Can't Look Away Anymore: The Anguished Politics of Breast Cancer," *New York Times Magazine,* August 15, 1993, 25–27, 58–60. For additional discussions of the Matuschka cover story see Maren Klawiter, "Racing for the Cure, Walking Women, and Toxic Touring: Mapping Cultures of Action within the Bay Area Terrain of Breast Cancer," *Social Problems* 46, no. 1 (1999): 104–26; and Lisa Cartwright, "Community and the Public Body in Breast Cancer Media Activism," *Cultural Studies* 12, no. 2 (1998): 117–38.

3. Verta Taylor and Marieke Van Willigen, "Women's Self-Help and the Reconstruction of Gender: The Postpartum Support and Breast Cancer Movements," *Mobilization* 1, no. 2 (1996): 123–42.

4. Independent Sector, "America's Tradition of Giving and Volunteering," *GuideStar.org,* http://www.guidestar.org/news/features/tradition.jsp (accessed August 10, 2005).

5. Roberta Altman, *Waking Up/Fighting Back: The Politics of Breast Cancer* (Boston: Little, Brown, 1996); Sharon Batt, *Patient No More: The Politics of Breast Cancer* (Charlottetown, P.E.I.: Gynergy Books, 1994); Ulrike Boehmer, *The Personal and the Political: Women's Activism in Response to the Breast Cancer and AIDS Epidemics* (New York: SUNY Press, 2000); Maureen Hogan Casamayou, *The Politics of Breast Cancer* (Washington, D.C.: Georgetown University Press, 2001); Klawiter, "Racing for the Cure"; Maren Klawiter, "From Private Stigma to Global Assembly: Transforming the Terrain of Breast Cancer," in *Global Ethnography: Forces, Connections, and Imaginations in a Postmodern World,* ed. Michael Burawoy and others (Berkeley: University of California Press, 2000), 420–73; Ellen Leopold, *A Darker Ribbon: Breast Cancer, Women, and Their Doctors in the Twentieth Century* (Boston: Beacon Press, 1999); Barron Lerner, *The Breast Cancer Wars: Hope, Fear, and the Pursuit of a Cure in Twentieth Century America* (New York: Oxford University Press, 2001); Jennifer Myhre, "Medical Mavens: Gender, Science and the Consensus Politics of Breast Cancer Activism" (PhD diss., University of California, Davis, 2001); Alissa Solomon, "The Politics of Breast Cancer," *Camera Obscura* 29 (1992): 157–77;

Karen Stabiner, *To Dance with the Devil: The New War on Breast Cancer* (New York: Delacorte Press, 1997); Taylor and Van Willigen, "Women's Self-Help."

6. Leopold, *Darker Ribbon;* Lerner, *Breast Cancer Wars.*

7. Leopold, *Darker Ribbon,* 194.

8. The "second wave" is the term used to describe the upsurge in feminist activism in the late 1960s and 1970s.

9. Altman, *Waking Up/Fighting Back;* Leopold, *Darker Ribbon;* Lerner, *Breast Cancer Wars.*

10. Barbara Ehrenreich, "Welcome to Cancerland," *Harper's,* November 2001, 43–53; Klawiter, "From Private Stigma"; Rose Kushner, *Breast Cancer: A Personal History and Investigative Report* (New York: Harcourt Brace Jovanovich, 1975).

11. Leopold, *Darker Ribbon,* 237.

12. Klawiter, "From Private Stigma."

13. Unable to compete for funds in the increasingly cutthroat business of breast cancer advocacy, NABCO closed its doors in 2004.

14. Stabiner, *To Dance with the Devil,* 60.

15. Altman, *Waking Up/Fighting Back;* Gina Kolata, "Weighing Spending on Breast Cancer," *New York Times,* October 20, 1993, sec. C, 14; Stabiner, *To Dance with the Devil.*

16. Stabiner, *To Dance with the Devil.*

17. Kolata, "Weighing Spending"; Stabiner, *To Dance with the Devil.*

18. National Cancer Institute, *Fact Book,* 2004, http://www3.cancer.gov/admin/fmb/04Factbk.pdf.

19. Nancy Evans, *State of the Evidence: What Is the Connection between the Environment and Breast Cancer?* 3rd ed. (Breast Cancer Fund and Breast Cancer Action, 2004), http://www.bcaction.org/PDF/StateofEvidence.pdf.

20. American Cancer Society, *Cancer Facts & Figures* 2005, http://www.cancer.org/downloads/STT/CAFF2005f4PWSecured.pdf. In situ cancers are confined within the ducts or lobules of the breast and have not yet spread beyond where they first emerged. Almost all in situ cancers are treatable. Invasive cancers are those that have broken through the walls of the duct or lobule and into the fatty tissue of the breast.

21. A discussion of this debate is available at http://www.bcaction.org/Pages/GetInformed/FAQStatistics.html#Q2.

22. American Cancer Society, *Cancer Facts & Figures* 2005.

23. American Cancer Society, *Cancer Facts & Figures,* 2004, http://www.cancer.org/downloads/STT/CAFF_finalPWSecured.pdf.

24. The individual studies on this issue are too numerous to mention, so I have cited here a review of literature by JudyAnn Bigby and Michelle Holmes that appeared in a 2005 special issue of *Cancer Causes and Control:* "Cancer Disparities: Developing a Multidisciplinary Research Agenda," *Cancer Causes and Control* 16,

no. 1 (February 2005): 35–44. It should also be noted that socioeconomic status has been defined inconsistently (and therefore problematically in terms of the veracity of research findings) by income, education, insurance status, employment history, and more in this body of research.

25. Leopold, *Darker Ribbon.*

26. As Leopold notes in *Darker Ribbon,* this stands in contrast to the March of Dimes, the volunteer-run organization established in 1938 by Franklin Delano Roosevelt, which was representative of a much broader cross-section of the U.S. population and which succeeded in funding research that eventually led to the eradication of polio as well as in dispensing large amounts of money ($203 million between 1938 and 1956) toward the costs of medical treatment.

27. Lerner, *Breast Cancer Wars.* For additional research on the history of breast cancer, see James Olson, *Bathsheba's Breast: Women, Cancer, and History* (Baltimore, Md.: Johns Hopkins University Press, 2002).

28. There have been several powerful critiques of the American Cancer Society's (ACS) breast cancer support program, Reach for Recovery: Cartwright, "Community and the Public Body"; Audre Lorde, *The Cancer Journals* (San Francisco: Spinster's Ink, 1980); Solomon, "The Politics of Breast Cancer." These pieces are more focused, however, on the individualizing and heternormative logic of this program, rather than the politics of charity. Reach for Recovery (R4R) was developed by breast cancer patient Therese Lasser in 1952 and was based on the then radically different idea that women who had experienced breast cancer could provide a special kind of emotional support for women newly in recovery. When ACS officially adopted the program in 1969, certain topics—such as family relationships, doctors, and the scar itself—were placed off limits for discussion. Instead, volunteers were supposed to convince women with mastectomies that they did not have a handicap but, in the words of Cartwright, "a condition from which they can recover—given the right attitude, clothes, and a prosthesis" (122). For feminist critics, R4R epitomizes broader, pre-1990s, social attitudes to breast cancer in that it requires women to cover up and depoliticize not just their missing or altered breast but also the personal and cultural struggles bound up with the experience of breast cancer. With the exception of Klawiter's "Racing for the Cure," which offers a comparative analysis of three cancer walks in the San Francisco Bay area (the Susan G. Komen Foundation's Race for the Cure, the Women and Cancer Walk, and the Toxic Tour of the Cancer Industry), when writing on the breast cancer movement does discuss the role of philanthropic organizations, it tends not to acknowledge or explore the distinction between breast cancer activism that focuses primarily on fund-raising for research, screening, and education and that which focuses primarily on political action designed to bring about change in established modes of addressing the disease.

29. Ford Motor Company, "Melissa's Story," http://www.fordvehicles.com/thecause/Melissa/.

30. Ehrenreich, "Welcome to Cancerland," 45.

31. National Breast Cancer Awareness Month, www.nbcam.org.

32. Ford Motor Company, "Ford Turns Up Volume to Raise Money to Fight Breast Cancer in 11th Year of Komen Sponsorship," news release, September 28, 2005, http://media.ford.com/newsroom/feature_display.cfm?release=21668.

33. Raymond Williams, *Keywords: A Vocabulary of Culture and Society* (London: Fontana, 1976).

34. My account of the history of the pink ribbon is based largely on Sandy Fernandez, "Pretty in Pink: The Life and Times of the Ribbon That Ties Breast Cancer to Corporate Giving," *MAMM,* June/July 1998, 52, 54–55, 64.

35. Research by Gerald Parsons, a folklorist and librarian at the American Folklife Center, suggests a more complex history. He dates the emergence of the ribbon as a symbol of hope and compassion to a 1950s folk legend about a prisoner returning home. Parsons, "How the Yellow Ribbon Became a National Folk Symbol," The American Folk Life Center, http://www.loc.gov/folklife/ribbons/ribbons.html.

36. Marita Sturken, *Tangled Memories: The Vietnam War, the AIDS Epidemic, and the Politics of Remembering* (Berkeley: University of California Press, 1997), 173.

37. Breast Cancer Action, "Why Do We Say 'Cancer Sucks'?" Breast Cancer Action, Newsletter 77, Summer 2003, http://www.bcaction.org/Pages/SearchablePages/2003Newsletters/Newsletter077G.html.

38. Jesse Green, "The Year of the Ribbon," *New York Times,* May 3, 1992, sec. V, 7.

39. Lisa Duggan, *The Twilight of Equality? Neoliberalism, Cultural Politics, and the Attack on Democracy* (New York: Beacon Press, 2003), xi. For additional discussions of the key features of neoliberalism, see Jean Comaroff and John L. Comaroff, *Millennial Capitalism and the Culture of Neoliberalism* (Durham, N.C.: Duke University Press, 2000); Noam Chomsky, *Profit over People: Neoliberalism and Global Order* (New York: Seven Stories Press, 1998); Nikolas Rose, *Powers of Freedom: Reframing Political Thought* (Cambridge: Cambridge University Press, 1999).

40. For a critical analysis of the relationship between the discourse of "community," nonprofit organizations, and capitalism, see Miranda Joseph, *Against the Romance of Community* (Minneapolis: University of Minnesota Press, 2002).

41. George [H. W.] Bush, "Two Presidents: One Goal," *USA Weekend,* April 25–27, 1997, 5.

42. Rose, *Powers of Freedom,* 166.

43. Mimi Hall and Bill Nichols, "Clinton: Citizenship Means Giving, Volunteerism Should Define USA, He Says," *USA Today,* April 25, 1997, A12.

44. Jack Bratich, Jeremy Packer, and Cameron McCarthy, eds., *Foucault, Cultural Studies, and Governmentality* (New York: SUNY Press, 2003), 17.

45. Rose, *Powers of Freedom,* 166.

46. Bratich, Packer, and McCarthy, *Foucault, Cultural Studies, and Governmentality,* 8.

47. Although the book is in many ways indebted to Foucauldian explanations of the neoliberal transformation of society, it also seeks to go beyond the rather totalizing accounts of this transformation, which, in Larry Grossberg's words, constitute neoliberalism as "too much of an intentionalist project, and too much of a singular model." See "Mapping the Intersections of Foucault and Cultural Studies: An Interview with Lawrence Grossberg and Toby Miller," by Jeremy Packer, in *Foucault, Cultural Studies, and Governmentality,* ed. Bratich, Packer, and McCarthy, 33. For Foucauldian analyses of neoliberalism, see Graham Burchell, Colin Gordon, and Peter Miller, eds., *The Foucault Effect: Studies in Governmentality* (Chicago: University of Chicago Press, 1991); Barbara Cruikshank, *The Will to Empower: Democratic Citizens and Other Subjects* (Ithaca, N.Y.: Cornell University Press, 1999); Rose, *Powers of Freedom.*

48. Bratich, Packer, and McCarthy, *Foucault, Cultural Studies, and Governmentality,* 8.

1. A Dream Cause

1. John Davidson, "Cancer Sells," *Working Woman,* May, 1997, 36. The Susan G. Komen Foundation is the largest private funder of breast cancer research in the United States. It was founded by Nancy Brinker in 1982, in memory of her sister who died of the disease. The foundation is best known for its national network of 5K runs, the Race for the Cure, which is discussed in detail in chapter 2.

2. According to Sandy Fernandez, in 1998, Carol Cone of Cone Communications told *MAMM* magazine that eighty to one hundred nationally recognized companies were involved in breast cancer marketing.

3. Lisa Belkin, "How Breast Cancer Became This Year's Hot Charity," *New York Times Magazine,* December 22, 1996, 40–46, 52, 55–56.

4. Stuart Ewen, *Captains of Consciousness: Advertising and the Social Roots of Consumer Culture* (New York: McGraw-Hill, 1976), 12. It is important to note here that corporate philanthropy and cause-related marketing are not synonymous, even if, as I argue, most giving is now carried out with markets in mind. Cause-related marketing campaigns are usually devised and managed by marketing departments, often in conjunction with philanthropy departments, but not every act of giving by a corporation is harnessed to a marketing campaign.

5. *A. P. Smith Manufacturing Co. v. Barlow,* 13 N.J. 154 (1953); Sophia Muirhead,

Corporate Contributions: The View from 50 Years (New York: Conference Board, 1999); John Yankey, "Corporate Support of Nonprofit Organizations," in *Corporate Philanthropy at the Crossroads,* ed. Dwight Burlingame and Dennis Young (Indianapolis: Indiana University Press, 1996), 7–22.

6. Muirhead, *Corporate Contributions.*

7. Jerome Himmelstein, "Corporate Philanthropy and Business Power," in Burlingame and Young, *Corporate Philanthropy,* 144–57.

8. Prior to the 1960s, corporations did not publicize their contributions. But during the social unrest of this decade and in specific response to activists who challenged corporate America on its environmental and hiring practices, among other things, corporations gradually decided to abandon anonymity in giving.

9. John Dienhart, "Charitable Investments: A Strategy for Improving the Business Environment," *Journal of Business Ethics* 7, nos. 1–2 (1988): 63; Peter Drucker, "The New Meaning of Corporate Social Responsibility," *California Management Review* 26 (1984): 59; Muirhead, *Corporate Contributions;* Yankey, "Corporate Support of Nonprofit Organizations"; M. Zetlin, "Companies Find Profit in Corporate Philanthropy," *Management Review* 79, no. 12 (1990): 10.

10. Elizabeth Boris, "The Nonprofit Sector in the 1990's," in *Philanthropy and the Nonprofit Sector in a Changing America,* ed. Charles Clotfelter and Thomas Ehrlich (Bloomington: Indiana University Press, 1999), 2.

11. Ronald Reagan, "Remarks at the Annual Meeting of the National Alliance of Business," *Weekly Compilation of Presidential Documents* 17, no. 4 (1981): 1085.

12. Hayden Smith, "Corporate Contributions in the year 2000," in *The Future of the Nonprofit Sector: Challenges, Changes and Policy Considerations,* ed. Virginia Hodgkinson and Richard Lyman (San Francisco: Jossey-Bass, 1989), 315–40. Changes to the tax code were made through the passing of the Economic Recovery Tax Act in 1981. Hayden Smith argues that these changes had a significant impact on corporate giving, at least in the short term. For 1982, there was a 22.4 percent increase in the number of companies reporting contributions equal to 5 percent or more of net income and a 38.4 percent increase in the average amount of their contributions. The total contributions of companies reporting 5 percent or more increased from 25.5 percent of total giving reported by all corporations in 1981 to 37.7 percent in 1982.

13. Michael Katz, *In the Shadow of the Poorhouse: A Social History of Welfare in America* (New York: Basic Books, 1996). Katz argues that escalation of government contracts for services with the private sector in the 1970s had made the voluntary sector more dependent on public sources of funding; cutbacks in public funds, therefore, left voluntary agencies with less money to spend.

14. Muirhead, *Corporate Contributions.* Founded in 1916, the Conference Board is a business membership and research nonprofit organization dedicated to helping businesses strengthen their performance.

15. Kirsten Grønbjerg and Steven Rathgeb Smith, "Nonprofit Organizations and Public Policies in the Delivery of Human Services," in *Philanthropy and the Nonprofit Sector,* ed. Clotfelter and Ehrlich, 139–71; Muirhead, *Corporate Contributions;* Lester Salamon and Alan Abramson, *The Federal Budget and the Nonprofit Sector* (Washington, D.C: Urban Institute Press, 1982); Zetlin, "Companies Find Profit."

16. Reynold Levy and Frank Oviatt, "Corporate Philanthropy," in *Experts in Action: Inside Public Relations,* ed. Bill Cantor (White Plains, N.Y.: Longman, 1998), 126–38; Brian O'Connell, *America's Voluntary Spirit: A Book of Readings* (New York: Foundations Center, 1983); James Shannon, *The Corporate Contributions Handbook* (San Francisco: Jossey-Bass, 1991).

17. O'Connell, *America's Voluntary Spirit,* 386.

18. Muirhead, *Corporate Contributions,* 36.

19. Ibid., 35, 36.

20. Shannon, *Corporate Contributions Handbook,* ix.

21. Lastra, quoted in Muirhead, *Corporate Contributions,* 41.

22. Muirhead, *Corporate Contributions,* 41.

23. Dienhart, *Charitable Investments,* 64.

24. Drucker, "Corporate Social Responsibility."

25. Shannon, *Corporate Contributions Handbook,* ix.

26. Craig Smith, "Desperately Seeking Data: Why Research Is Crucial to Corporate Philanthropy," in *Corporate Philanthropy,* ed. Burlingame and Young, 1.

27. These include manuals detailing the components of a profitable contributions program, qualitative and quantitative methods to measure outcomes and performance, the creation of new courses in philanthropy (such as the yearlong Rockefeller Foundation Philanthropy Workshop), and the publication of numerous new magazines and online publications like *GuideStar,* which has joined more established journals such as the *Chronicle of Philanthropy* and the *Nonprofit Times.*

28. Myra Alperson, *Corporate Giving Strategies That Add Business Value* (New York: Conference Board, 1995); Reynold Levy, "Corporate Philanthropy Comes of Age: Its Size, Its Import, Its Future," in *Philanthropy and the Nonprofit Sector,* ed. Clotfelter and Ehrlich, 99–121; Muirhead, *Corporate Contributions.*

29. John Davidson, "Cancer Sells," *Working Woman,* May 1997, 37.

30. Alperson, *Corporate Giving Strategies;* Davidson, "Cancer Sells"; Jacqueline Foley, "Picking a Philanthropic Partner," *Marketing Magazine,* September 7, 1998, 16; John Graham, "'Doing Good' Is Good and Bad for Business," *SuperVision,* July 1994, 11–13; Muirhead, *Corporate Contributions;* Jennifer Mullen, "Performance-Based Corporate Philanthropy: How 'Giving Smart' Can Further Corporate Goals," *Public Relations Quarterly,* Summer 1997, 42–48; Myra Stark, "Brand Aid: Cause Effective," *Brandweek,* February 22, 1999, 20–22.

31. Nancy Arnott, "Marketing with a Passion," *Sales and Marketing Management*

146, no. 1 (1994): 64–71; Hamish Pringle and Marjorie Thompson, *Brand Spirit: How Cause Related Marketing Builds Brands* (New York: Wiley, 1999).

32. Pringle and Thompson, *Brand Spirit,* 12.

33. Ibid., 14.

34. Mullen, "Performance-Based Corporate Philanthropy," 42.

35. Jerry Welsh, "Good Cause, Good Business," *Harvard Business Review* 21 (1999): 24. As the creators of the 1983 American Express Campaign to raise funds for the renovation of the Statue of Liberty, Welsh Marketing Associates of New York are widely regarded as the founders of cause-related marketing.

36. Mullen, "Performance-Based Corporate Philanthropy," 43.

37. Alperson, *Corporate Giving Strategies,* 10.

38. Pringle and Thompson, *Brand Spirit.*

39. Jeff Green, "Brand Builders," *Brandweek,* October 4, 32, 34. The fact that Reebok spent over $10 million to promote and produce Amnesty International's Human Rights Now! Tour in 1988, which amounted to over 90 percent of its entire marketing budget for that year, indicates the level to which corporations view cause-related marketing as a good investment (see Pringle and Thompson, *Brand Spirit*).

40. Stark, "Brand Aid," 20.

41. Pringle and Thompson, *Brand Spirit,* 23.

42. Ibid., xxi, 12.

43. Davidson, "Cancer Sells"; Pringle and Thompson, *Brand Spirit;* Stark, "Brand Aid."

44. Pringle and Thompson, *Brand Spirit,* xxi–xxii.

45. Ibid., 12.

46. Robert Putnam, "Bowling Alone: America's Declining Social Capital," *Journal of Democracy* 6, no. 1 (1995): 65–78; Putnam, *Bowling Alone: The Collapse and Revival of American Community* (New York: Simon and Schuster, 2000). See also Robert Bellah, *Habits of the Heart: Individualism and Commitment in American Life* (Berkeley: University of California Press, 1985).

47. Pringle and Thompson, *Brand Spirit,* 32.

48. Ibid.

49. Ibid., 12.

50. Ibid., xxii–xxiii, 4.

51. The list represents only a small sampling of the forty-nine companies that staged fund-raising events for the foundation in 2005, according to their Web site, http://www.komen.org.

52. Davidson, "Cancer Sells"; Debra Goldman, "Illness as a Metaphor," *Adweek,* November 3, 1997, 70; Stark, "Brand Aid."

53. Mazurki, quoted in Davidson, "Cancer Sells," 4.

54. Sandy Fernandez, "Pretty in Pink: The Life and Times of the Ribbon That Ties Breast Cancer to Corporate Giving," *MAMM*, June/July 1998, 52, 54–55, 64.

55. When market concerns drive philanthropic practice, chosen causes come and go. The relationship between the NFL and the Komen Foundation ended in 2001. An NFL official told me that both parties were refocusing their marketing efforts, although it was possible that the relationship might be resumed in the future. He also noted that the partnership was regarded as a success by both organizations.

56. Becky Yerak, "Lion's Share Market with Women: Alpha Males Move Over," *Detroit News*, January 7, 2000, sec. B, 1.

57. National Football League, "NFL Sponsors Race for the Cure," news release, April 19, 1999.

58. Ibid.

59. Jim Auchmutey, "The Scene: A Beefy Sport with a Heart," *Atlanta Journal and Constitution*, January 28, 2000, sec. E, 2; National Football League, "NFL Players Spend Mother's Day on the Road at Komen Race for the Cure Events," news release, May 3, 1999. Following the signing of the agreement, NFL officials, players, coaches, and spouses made heavily promoted appearances at a range of Komen events. Moreover, in the week leading up to the Super Bowl, NFL players offered a class for breast cancer survivors affiliated with the Susan G. Komen Foundation who wished to "know more about football."

60. Yerak, "Lion's Share," 3.

61. National Football League, "Real Men Wear Pink: NFL Encourages Women and Men to Join the Fight against Breast Cancer," news release, October 10, 1999. Each of five spots featured a different, high-profile player—Tony Gonzalez, tight end with the Kansas City Chiefs; Jamal Anderson, then running back with the Atlanta Falcons; Hardy Nickerson, then linebacker of the Tampa Bay Buccaneers; Kordell Stewart, then quarterback for the Pittsburgh Steelers; and Jason Sehorn, then defensive back of the New York Giants. The sixth spot was a compilation with music but no voice-overs.

62. Ibid.

63. Cheryl Cole, "American Jordan: P.L.A.Y., Consensus and Punishment," *Sociology of Sport Journal* 13 (1996): 336–97.

64. Interview with Jeff Benedict by Armen Keteyian, "Crime Season: An Explosive New Book Attacks," *Sport*, October 1998, 32.

65. The "character discourse" in the realm of sport is not a new invention, nor does it get mobilized simply in relation to criminal behavior. In fact, mainstream sports in the United States and elsewhere have been historically narrated as bastions of fair play, discipline, self-betterment, and character building, ideals that extensive research in the history and sociology of sport have shown to be deeply

layered with exclusions and norms based on class, gender, and race. See Susan Cahn, *Coming on Strong: Gender and Sexuality in Twentieth Century Women's Sport* (New York: Free Press, 1994).

66. Peter Attner, "Prospects or Suspects?" *Sporting News,* April 21, 1997, sec. S, 2.

67. Keteyian, "Crime Season," 32. Out of a sample of 509 NFL players on the 1996–97 roster, John Benedict and Donald Yaeger claim that 21.4 percent had been arrested for more than petty crimes. Benedict and Yaeger, *Pros and Cons: The Criminals Who Play in the NFL* (New York: Warner, 1999).

68. Keteyian, "Crime Season," 33.

69. Lewis was acquitted in June 2000. In January 2001, Rae Carruth was found guilty of conspiracy to commit murder, shooting into an occupied vehicle, and using an instrument to destroy an unborn child and was sentenced to eighteen to twenty-four years in prison.

70. Interview with Paul Tagliabue by Frank Deford, *Morning Edition,* National Public Radio, February 16, 2000.

71. Attner, "Prospects or Suspects?"; Kevin Baker, "NFL: National Felons League," *Wall Street Journal,* February 4, 2000, sec. A, 18; Jeff Duncan "Despite Lip Service, Teams Can't Keep from Drafting Questionable Characters," *Times-Picayune,* April 23, 2000, sec. C, 4; Mike Freeman, "N.F.L. and Union Weigh Players' Violent Acts," *New York Times,* March 26, 2000, sec. 8, 2; Mike Freeman, "Stains from the Police Blotter Leave N.F.L. Embarrassed," *New York Times,* January 9, 2000, sec. 8, 4; Patrick Hruby, "Tests of Character," *Insight,* May 1, 2000, 28–29; Gary Myers, "A Dubious Cast of Characters," *New York Daily News,* April 17, 2000, 64; Katherine Smith, "Off-Field Image May Stain the NFL Image," *Tampa Tribune,* May 15, 2000, 1.

72. Diane Shah, "Leagues Try to Protect, Educate Players," *Chicago Sun-Times,* May 7, 2000, 113.

73. Freeman, "N.F.L. and Union."

74. Jarret Bell, "Friends Come to Lewis' Defense," *USA Today,* May 15, 2000, sec. C, 1.

75. Ibid.

76. Tom Goldman, "Jury Selection to Begin Today in Murder Trial of Pro Footballer Ray Lewis," *Morning Edition,* National Public Radio, 2000.

77. Myers, "A Dubious Cast."

78. Judy Battista, "N.F.L. Draft: Troubled Pasts Don't Worry Jets," *New York Times,* April 17, 2000, sec. D, 7; Duncan, "Despite Lip Service"; Myers, "A Dubious Cast."

79. Myers, "A Dubious Cast."

80. Clinton, quoted in Mimi Hall and Bill Nichols, "Clinton: Citizenship Means

Giving, Volunteerism Should Define USA, He Says," *USA Today,* April 25, 1997, sec. A, 12.

81. It is also worthwhile noting that the Real Men Wear Pink campaign emerged very soon after the impeachment of Bill Clinton due to his presumed lack of character, and the Lewis and Carruth stories appeared around the time that George W. Bush was mobilizing yet another character discourse during his presidential run both by attacking the character of his opponent and that of the Democratic Party and by placing character development among citizens, particularly children, at the center of his campaign. Character discourses, in other words, have been ubiquitous during this era.

82. Breast Cancer Action, "Thinking beyond Pink," Breast Cancer Action, Newsletter 75, January/February 2003, http://www.bcaction.org/Pages/SearchablePages/2003Newsletters/Newsletter075H.html.

83. Breast Cancer Action, "Think Before You Pink," www.thinkbeforeyoupink.org.

84. Barbara Brenner, "Our Silence Will Not Protect You," Breast Cancer Action, Newsletter 79, November/December 2003, http://www.bcaction.org/Pages/SearchablePages/2003Newsletters/Newsletter079B.html.

85. For a detailed discussion of the Avon Walk for Breast Cancer, see chapter 2.

86. Brenner, "Our Silence."

87. Ibid.

2. Doing Good by Running Well

1. Susan G. Komen Breast Cancer Foundation, "Pathways to a Promise: 2003–2004 Annual Report," Susan G. Komen Breast Cancer Foundation, http://www.komen.org/stellent/groups/public/@dallas/documents/-komen_site_documents/2003-2004annualreport.pdf.

2. For an analysis that compares the Race for the Cure to other collective responses to the breast cancer epidemic, see Maren Klawiter, "Racing for the Cure, Walking Women, and Toxic Touring: Mapping Cultures of Action within the Bay Area Terrain of Breast Cancer," *Social Problems* 46, no. 1 (1999): 104–26.

3. The 1999 Komen Race for the Cure series was "presented nationally" by J. C. Penney and "sponsored nationally" by American Airlines, Ford Motor Company, Johnson & Johnson, the National Football League, New Balance Athletic Shoes, Pier 1 Imports, and Tropicana Pure Premium orange juice. Sponsors specific to the Washington, D.C., race included Bristol Myers Squibb Oncology, Freddie Mac, Safeway, Konica, Schering-Plough, Washington Area Ford Dealers, Motorola, Genentech Biooncology, Chevy Chase Bank, Microsoft, The

Fitness Company, Papa John's Pizza, Meridian Moving and Storage, Prudential, Monsanto, Mosaic Foundation, Nestlé, Fluor Corporation, Les Halles Brasserie, the *Washington Post,* Soft Rock 97.1, *Washingtonian* magazine, *Families* magazine, *Metro* magazine, *Latina Style* magazine, *Shape (Jump)* magazine, Next Generation Network, WTOP 107.7 FM Top News Nonstop, NBC television (D.C.), Eli Lilly, Fresh Fields Whole Foods Market, Nordstrom, SalomonSmithBarney, Kodak, Target, Amgen, ABB, CNG, First Union, Capital One, the Ann Hand Collection, El Paso Energy, Gateway Computers, Greenberg Traurig Attorneys at Law, Marmot Foundation, Zeneca Pharmaceuticals, Fannie Mae Foundation, Open MRI, BlueCross BlueShield, NFL, Proctor and Gamble, Merck, Hecht's, Union Pacific Corporation, International Paper, Pfizer, Deer Park Spring Water, Romano's Macaroni Grill, Tanaka Memorial Foundation, and Precision Marketing Inc.

4. Nancy Statchen, "Why Am I Running?" online message board, Susan G. Komen Breast Cancer Foundation, July 1998, www.komen.org.

5. The survivors were of a variety of ages, although the majority appeared to be middle-aged. There were a handful of women who had lost their hair and who were not wearing wigs, and a few more who donned turbans. Most of the survivors, however, wore hair on their heads and lots of makeup. The overwhelming majority of participants in the race were white. There was a small (approximately forty) and prominent (in part because speakers at the rallies drew attention to them) contingent of African American women from the breast cancer support group Rise Sister Rise, which was sponsored by the Komen Foundation and GlaxoWellcome pharmaceuticals.

6. Audre Lorde, *The Cancer Journals* (San Francisco: Spinster's Ink, 1980), 16.

7. For evidence of the silence of the Komen Foundation on the relationship between environmental factors and breast cancer incidence, see their Web site, www.komen.org; Nancy Brinker, *The Race Is One Step at a Time* (Arlington, Tex.: Summit, 1995); and the foundation's triannual newsletter *Frontline* (recent issues are available on their Web site, http://www.komen.org/intradoc-cgi/idc_cgi_isapi.dll?IdcService=SS_GET_PAGE&ssDocName=FrontlineNewsletter). The Komen Foundation's primary agenda is to encourage women to undertake early detection (via mammography, self-exam, and regular checkups) and, more recently, risk evaluation.

8. James Patterson, *The Dread Disease: Cancer and Modern American Culture* (Cambridge: Harvard University Press, 1987).

9. Sharon Batt, *Patient No More: The Politics of Breast Cancer* (Charlottetown, P.E.I.: Gynergy Books, 1994); Judy Brady, *1 in 3: Women with Cancer Confront an Epidemic* (San Francisco: Cleis Press, 1991); Samuel Epstein, *The Politics of Cancer Revisted* (New York: East Ridge Press, 1998); Ellen Leopold, *A Darker Ribbon: Breast Cancer, Women, and Their Doctors in the Twentieth Century* (Boston: Beacon Press, 1999); Alissa Solomon, "The Politics of Breast Cancer," *Camera Obscura* 29 (1992): 157–77.

10. Nikolas Rose, *Powers of Freedom: Reframing Political Thought* (Cambridge: Cambridge University Press, 1999).

11. Mary Ann Swissler, "The Marketing of Breast Cancer," September 16, 2002, http://www.alternet.org/envirohealth/14014/. In an investigative report for *Southern Exposure* magazine (reprinted on www.alternet.org), Swissler notes that Rae Evans is the major lobbyist in Washington, D.C., for the Komen Foundation. According to Swissler, she has "little experience or interest in grassroots advocacy" and "doubles as a lobbyist for Nancy Brinker's husband, restaurant magnate and polo champion Norman Brinker of Brinker International."

12. Evans was presumably referring to the part of King's speech that read as follows: "I have a dream that one day, down in Alabama, with its vicious racists, with its governor having his lips dripping with the words of interposition and nullification; one day right down in Alabama little black boys and black girls will be able to join hands with little white boys and white girls as sisters and brothers."

13. Ruth Frankenberg, *White Women, Race Matters: The Social Construction of Whiteness* (Minneapolis: University of Minnesota Press, 1993), 14.

14. Birgit Brander Rasmussen and others, eds., *The Making and Unmaking of Whiteness* (Durham, N.C.: Duke University Press, 2001), 5.

15. See, for example, my discussion of the Patients' Bill of Rights in the "Ribbon and the Monument" section of this chapter.

16. Lauren Berlant, *The Queen of America Goes to Washington City: Essays on Sex and Citizenship* (Durham, N.C.: Duke University Press, 1997), 187.

17. Ibid.

18. Marita Sturken, *Tangled Memories: The Vietnam War, the Aids Epidemic, and the Politics of Remembering* (Berkeley: University of California Press, 1997).

19. Barbara Christian, "The Crime of Innocence," in *The Good Citizen,* ed. David Batstone and Eduardo Mendieta (New York: Routledge, 1999), 51–64.

20. Berlant, *Queen of America,* 3.

21. Ibid.

22. Graham Burchell, Colin Gordon, and Peter Miller, *The Foucault Effect: Studies in Governmentality* (Chicago: University of Chicago Press, 1991); Barbara Cruikshank, *The Will to Empower: Democratic Citizens and Other Subjects* (Ithaca, N.Y.: Cornell University Press, 1999); Rose, Powers of Freedom.

23. Swissler, "Marketing of Breast Cancer."

24. Michael Seltzer, telephone conversation with author, October 4, 1999. My history of the Freedom from Hunger marches and the rise of the thon is indebted to Seltzer, a leader in the field of nonprofit management and philanthropy. Seltzer worked as East Coast field director of the Freedom from Hunger Foundation between 1969 and 1972 and was generous in sharing with me his understanding of this history.

25. This information was provided in my telephone conversation with Michael Seltzer (ibid.), but I have been unable to find the relevant articles.

26. Cheryl Cole and Amy Hribar, "Celebrity Feminism: Nike Style (Post-Fordism, Transcendence, and Consumer Power)," *Sociology of Sport Journal* 12 (1995): 347–69; Jeremy Howell, "A Revolution in Motion: Advertising and the Politics of Nostalgia," *Sociology of Sport Journal* 8 (1991): 258–71; Alan Ingham, "From Public Issue to Personal Trouble: Well-Being and the Fiscal Crisis of the State," *Sociology of Sport Journal* 2 (1985): 43–55; Susan Jeffords, *Hard Bodies: Hollywood Masculinity in the Reagan Era* (New Brunswick, N.J.: Rutgers University Press, 1994).

27. Howell, "Revolution in Motion"; Jeffords, *Hard Bodies.*

28. Cole and Hribar, "Celebrity Feminism."

29. Mike Featherstone, *Consumer Culture and Postmodernism* (Newbury Park, Calif.: Sage, 1991); Howell, "Revolution in Motion"; Ingham, "From Public Issue."

30. Lisa Hamm-Greenawalt, "Cause and Effect," *Runner's World* 35 (1999): 28.

31. Cesar, quoted in Lena Williams, "New Charity Strategy: Get Up and Go," *New York Times,* May 7, 1995, sec. I, 32.

32. Liquori, quoted in ibid. The Leukemia Society of America changed its name to the Leukemia and Lymphoma Society in 2000.

33. Interview with Nancy Brinker by Norma Libman, "Leading the Way," *Chicago Tribune,* May 26, 1996, sec. 13, 3.

34. Ibid.

35. Beth Hagman, "A Higher Purpose," *Fitness Runner,* Fall 1999, 6–17, 20, 22.

36. Williams, "New Charity Strategy," 32.

37. Interview conducted via e-mail, September 1999, name withheld.

38. For a discussion of the history of Avon's involvement with gender politics and women's health, see chapter 4.

39. Barbara Brenner, "Exercise Your Mind," Breast Cancer Action, Newsletter 58, March/April, 2000, http://www.bcaction.org/Pages/SearchablePages/2000Newsletters/Newsletter058B.html.

40. Ibid.

41. Barbara Brenner, "Ding, Dong: Activists Call on Avon," Breast Cancer Action, Newsletter 69, January/February, 2002, http://www.bcaction.org/Pages/SearchablePages/2002Newsletters/Newsletter069B.html.

42. Ibid.

43. Barbara Brenner, "Breast Cancer Activists Follow the Money to Avon Shareholder Meeting," Breast Cancer Action, Newsletter 72, July/August, 2002, http://www.bcaction.org/Pages/SearchablePages/2002Newsletters/Newsletter072E.html.

44. Ibid.

45. I conducted research at the Avon Walk for Breast Cancer in Boston on May 15 and 16, 2004.

46. Brenner, "Breast Cancer Activists."

47. Convio, Inc., "Convio Helps 'Weekend to End Breast Cancer' Walks Raise More Than $21 million (CDN) in Less Than a Year," news release, November 4, 2004, http://www.charitychannel.com/publish/templates/?a=1459&z=34; http://www.causeforce.com.

48. Ulysses Torassa, "Fundraiser Flap Irks Activists: Komen Breast Cancer Walk Competes with Avon's," *San Francisco Chronicle,* June 28, 2003, http://www .aegis.com/news/sc/2003/SC030621.html.

3. Stamping Out Breast Cancer

1. The cost was increased from 40 to 45 cents in 2002.

2. The Department of Defense's involvement in breast cancer came about in the wake of the Cold War and the "firewall" that had been erected by Congress during that era to protect defense spending so that, in effect, no money could be taken from defense funds and spent on domestic programs. In FY 1993, breast cancer activists successfully campaigned to encourage members of Congress to vote to transfer $210 million of DOD money to breast cancer research. This followed a more limited campaign in FY 1992, which saw an appropriation of $25 million targeted to a reluctant DOD to conduct research on the screening and diagnosis of breast cancer among military women and dependents. Since that time, this limited project has grown into the Congressionally Directed Medical Research Programs (CDMRP) and has expanded to become second only to the National Cancer Institute as a source of funding for breast cancer research and a leading site of study into a range of other diseases.

3. U.S. Postal Service, "Fundraising Stamp (Semipostal Stamp Program)," http://www.usps.com/communications/community/semipostals.htm; National Cancer Institute, "Breast Cancer Stamp Will Fund Premalignancy Research," http://www.cancer.gov/ncicancerbulletin/NCI_Cancer_Bulletin_020706/page9; Department of Defense, "Fact Sheet: The Breast Cancer Postage Stamp and the Involvement of the Department of Defense Breast Cancer Research Program," http://cdmrp.army.mil/pubs/factsheets/bcstampfactsheet .htm.

4. *Semipostal Authorization Act,* HR 4437, 106th Cong., 2d sess., *Congressional Record* 146 (July 17, 2000): H 6068.

5. A semipostal stamp is one that has its net proceeds above the cost of first-class postage (minus the postal service's reasonable costs) earmarked for specified purposes.

6. George W. Bush, "Address to the Nation," November 8, 2001, http://www .whitehouse.gov/news/releases/2001/11/20011108-13.html.

7. Gina Kolata, "Vying for the Breast Vote," *New York Times,* November 3, 1996, sec. 4, 5.

8. Kolata, "Vying"; Carol Weisman, *Women's Health Care: Activist Traditions and Institutions* (Baltimore, Md.: Johns Hopkins University Press, 1998), 206.

9. Mary Vavrus, "From Women of the Year to 'Soccer Moms': The Case of the Incredible Shrinking Women," *Political Communication* 17, no. 2 (2000): 193–213.

10. Ibid., 193.

11. Kolata, "Vying."

12. Tucker Carlson, "Lauch 'n' load," *Weekly Standard,* October 12, 1998, 16.

13. Joyce Purnick, "Exploiting Breast Cancer for Politics," *New York Times,* March 6, 2000, sec. B, 1.

14. See National Breast Cancer Coalition, www.natlbcc.org.

15. The idea that less government is better continued to characterize the administration of George W. Bush, even if this same administration created one of the "biggest" governments, in terms of spending and surveillance and intrusion, in U.S. history. Although, as Jim Vanderhei, writing for the *Washington Post,* suggests, "Bush maintains a stated desire to streamline the government" and has instigated three major tax cuts and cut nondefense spending, his administration is also responsible for the biggest annual budget spending increases in U.S. presidential history; the creation of the biggest federal bureaucracy, in the form of the Department of Homeland Security, since the 1947 creation of the Department of Defense; as well as new national restrictions in the realms of marriage, education, and litigation. Jim Vanderhei, "Blueprint Calls for Bigger, More Powerful Government," *Washington Post,* February 9, 2005, sec. A, 1; the Presidential Reporting Project, "Fact Checking the Bush Resume," Graduate School of Journalism, University of California, Berkeley, October 15, 2004, http://journalism.berkeley.edu/projects/election2004/reporting/archives/003344.html.

16. Nikolas Rose, *Powers of Freedom: Reframing Political Thought* (Cambridge: Cambridge University Press, 1999).

17. James Patterson, *The Dread Disease: Cancer and Modern American Culture* (Cambridge: Harvard University Press, 1987).

18. Ellen Leopold, "Switching Priorities in the Breast Cancer Fight," *Boston Globe,* October 20, 1999, sec. A, 19.

19. Patterson, *Dread Disease.*

20. June Goodfield, *The Siege of Cancer* (New York: Random House, 1975), 156.

21. Alison Mitchell, "Clinton Campaign Puts an Emphasis on Female Voters," *New York Times,* October 28, 1996, sec. A, 1, 16; Roxanne Roberts, "The First Lady's Women's Crusade," *Washington Post,* May 6, 1995, sec. D, 2; *Stamp Out Breast Cancer Act,* HR 1585, 105th Cong., 1st sess., *Congressional Record* 143 (July 22, 1997): H 5521; *Stamp Out Breast Cancer Act,* HR 1585, 105th Congress, 1st session, *Congressional Record* 143 (July 24, 1997): S 8040.

22. Roberts, "The First Lady's Women's Crusade."

23. Lauren Berlant, *The Queen of America Goes to Washington City: Essays on Sex and Citizenship* (Durham, N.C.: Duke University Press, 1997), 22.

24. A search of the LexisNexis Academic Universe index revealed that a total of 10 articles on the Breast and Cervical Cancer Treatment Act, which would provide Medicaid coverage for the treatment of low-income women, were published in the nation's major regional newspapers between the time the bill was first introduced, in March 1999, and May 2000, when the act passed through the House. In contrast, a total of 23 articles on the Stamp Out Breast Cancer Act were published between January 1997, when this bill was introduced into the House, and August 1997, when President Clinton signed it into law. Since that time, another 69 articles on the breast cancer stamp have been published in newspapers indexed through LexisNexis.

25. In an interview with NBCC's Government Relations Officer, I learned, in addition, that the organization did not support the legislation because according to original estimates, the stamp was projected to raise less than $500,000.

26. Lyn Alweis, "P.O. Rallies to Stamp Out Breast Cancer, *Denver Post,* April 29, 2000, sec. B, 2; Christine Bordelon, "Breast Cancer Stamp Unveiled In Kenner," *Times-Picayune,* October 28, 1999, sec. D, 1; "Cancer Research Stamp Being Celebrated," *Seattle Times,* March 16, 2000, sec. B, 3; "New Stamp Benefits Breast Cancer Research," *Times-Picayune,* October 21, 1999, sec. A, 1.

27. Diane Feinstein, "Help Stamp Out Breast Cancer," *San Francisco Chronicle,* October 13, 1998, sec. A, 21.

28. Berlant, *Queen of America,* 13.

29. Marina Dundjerski, "Congress Approves Stamp to Raise Research Money," *Chronicle of Philanthropy,* August 7, 1997, 26.

30. Feinstein, "Help Stamp," 21; P. Hong and T. Schultz, "Stamp to Fund Research on Breast Cancer," *Los Angeles Times,* May 9, 1998, sec. A, 20.

31. Fast Company, Fast 50, "Stamp Out Disease," http://www.fastcompany.com/fast50_02/people/trendsetters/32.html.

32. Feinstein, "Help Stamp," 21.

33. Ibid.; Hong and Schultz, "Stamp to Fund"; Sabin Russell, "Surgeon Puts Stamp on Breast Cancer," *San Francisco Chronicle,* May 9, 1998, sec. A, 1; Gregg Zoroya, "Politicians Look for the Stamp of Approval," *Los Angeles Times,* July 23, 1997, sec. E, 1.

34. Feinstein, "Help Stamp," 21.

35. Hong and Schultz, "Stamp to Fund," 20; Russell, "Surgeon Puts Stamp," 1.

36. Dundjerski, "Congress Approves," 26; Larry McKinnis, "U.S. Semi-Postal Issue Set: Surcharge Could Go to Charity or Breast Cancer Research," *Montreal Gazette,* October 4, 1997, sec. J, 3.

37. *Stamp Out Breast Cancer Act* (July 24, 1997): S 8040.

38. Bill McAllister, "Cancer Stamp May Lead to More Fundraisers," *Denver Post,* May 7, 2000, sec. A, 35.

39. McInnis, "U.S. Semi-Postal."

40. Russell, "Surgeon Puts Stamp," 1.

41. James Hayes, e-mail to dadlobby@juno.com mailing list, October 26, 1999.

42. Leopold, "Switching Priorities."

43. Rod Watson, "Great Idea! Let's Use Pennies on Postage Stamp to Make Lots of Government Optional," *Buffalo News,* May 22, 1997, 2B; "When Government Goes Begging," June 1, 1997, *Boston Globe,* sec. C, 6.

44. *Stamp Out Breast Cancer Act* (July 24, 1997): S 8040.

45. *Stamp Out Breast Cancer Act* (July 22, 1997): H 5521.

46. Ibid.

47. Ibid.

48. Ibid.

49. *Stamp Out Breast Cancer Act* (July 24, 1997): S 8040.

50. United States Postal Service, "Nation's First Breast Cancer Research 'Semi-postal' Stamp Issued at White House Ceremony," news release, July 29, 1998.

51. *Stamp Out Breast Cancer Act* (July 22, 1997): H 5521.

52. Rose, *Powers of Freedom.*

53. *Stamp Out Breast Cancer Act* (July 22, 1997): H 5521.

54. Ibid.

55. Ibid.

56. Senator Lauch Faircloth, "Victory for Breast Cancer," news release, August, 1997.

57. Margo Harakas, "Help Stamp Out Breast Cancer with 8 Cents," *Arizona Republic,* September 14, 1998, sec. D, 8.

58. Ibid.

59. Alweis, "P.O. Rallies"; Bordelon, "Breast Cancer Stamp Unveiled"; "Cancer Research Stamp Being Celebrated"; "New Stamp Benefits Breast Cancer Research."

60. *Stamp Out Breast Cancer Act* (July 22, 1997): H 5521.

61. Ibid.

62. Mitchell, "Clinton Campaign."

63. Roberts, "The First Lady's Women's Crusade."

64. Susan Ferraro, "You Can't Look Away Anymore: The Anguished Politics of Breast Cancer," *New York Times Magazine,* August 15, 1993, 25–27, 58–60.

65. John Davidson, "Cancer Sells," *Working Woman,* May 1997, 37.

66. Ibid, 37.

67. The relationship of the AIDS and breast cancer movements is discussed in detail in chapter 5.

68. For an account of the relationship between women voters, in particular,

and the reduction of electoral politics to a mode of consumption, see Vavrus, "From Women of the Year."

69. Jane Levere, "National Breast Cancer Awareness Month Has Inspired Extensive Corporate Advertising," *New York Times,* October 3, 1996, sec. D, 6.

70. National Breast Cancer Coalition, http://www.natlbcc.org.

71. The Breast and Cervical Treatment Act would provide Medicaid coverage for women diagnosed with breast or cervical cancer through the Center for Disease Control's Breast and Cervical Cancer Early Protection Program, which currently screens low-income women and then leaves them to scramble for treatment in an ad hoc system of charity care.

4. Imperial Charity

1. AstraZeneca, "The Redefining Hope and Beauty Campaign," news release, September 2004, http://www.hopeandbeauty.org/press_materials/RH&B%20 Backgrounder-Final.pdf.

2. Avon, "Avon 2002 Annual Report: Transforming," http://www.avoncompany .com/investor/annualreport/pdf/avp02areditorial.pdf.

3. Avon United Kingdom was actually the first Avon location to launch a breast cancer campaign. It did so in 1992, and Avon Canada, USA, and Puerto Rico took up the idea the following year.

4. I use the word "might" here because this part of my analysis is necessarily speculative given that I have not been able to investigate how Avon's endeavors are actually playing out in local contexts. Instead, the research sources for this chapter are drawn mostly from the Avon corporation itself. Based on these materials, I have been able to explore the strategies and tools it is using in its effort to shape the course of the disease, as well as its vision of the ideal consumer-subject who will participate in its philanthropic initiatives.

5. Fredric Jameson, "Notes on Globalization as a Philosophical Issue," in *The Culture of Globalization,* ed. Fredric Jameson and Masao Miyoshi (Durham, N.C.: Duke University Press, 1998), xiii.

6. The more central role played by corporate concerns in international relations of power has been accompanied by—and, through the lending policies of bodies such as the International Monetary Fund, has helped shape—a downsizing of public sector services worldwide.

7. Audris Tillman, *Corporate Contributions in 1999* (New York: Conference Board, 2000).

8. Anne Klepper, *Global Contributions of U.S. Corporations* (New York: Conference Board, 1993). Founded in 1916, the Conference Board is a business membership and research network nonprofit organization dedicated to helping businesses strengthen their performance.

9. Tillman, *Corporate Contributions*.

10. The Conference Board, "Corporate Citizenship Programs Gaining Attention," September 15, 2002, http://www.conference-board.org.

11. Nanette Byrnes, "Avon's New Calling," *Business Week*, September 18, 2000, 18. Of all direct salespeople in the United States, 72.5 percent are women, and 90 percent of direct sales agents work part-time, according to the Direct Selling Association, http://www.dsa.org.

12. Avon, "Avon 2003 Annual Report: Unleashing Growth," http://www.avoncompany.com/investor/annualreport/2003index.html; Byrnes, "Avon's New Calling."

13. Avon, "Avon 2003 Annual Report," 6.

14. Richard Bartlett, "There Is No Freedom without Free Enterprise" (speech given at the Academic Seminar on Direct Selling, São Paulo, Brazil, October 6, 1998), http://www.wfdsa.org/library/saopaulo.asp.

15. Byrnes, "Avon's New Calling."

16. Ibid.; Avon, http://www.avon.com/about/women/foundation/foundation.html.

17. Troy, quoted in Todd Kulik, *The Expanding Parameters of Global Corporate Citizenship* (New York: Conference Board, 2000), 7.

18. Ibid.

19. *BusinessWeek Online*, "2003 Global Brands Scoreboard," August 2003, http://bwnt.businessweek.com/brand/2003/index.asp.

20. See http://www.avon.com.

21. Samantha King, "Marketing Generosity: The Avon WorldWide Fund for Women's Health and the Reinvention of Global Corporate Citizenship," in *Sport and Corporate Nationalisms*, ed. David Andrews, Michael Silk, and C. L. Cole (New York: Berg, 2005), 83–108.

22. Avon, "Philanthropy," http://www.avoncompany.com/index.html.

23. I have been unable to find one reference to the fund on any of the hundreds of pages of materials on Avon's U.S. or international Web sites.

24. My research to date suggests that both the old and the new breast cancer campaign titles are translated into the majority language of the respective countries in which they are undertaken.

25. The Avon Foundation, "The Avon Foundation 2002 Annual Report," 5.

26. Jill Moffett, "Moving beyond the Ribbon: An Examination of Breast Cancer Advocacy in the U.S. and Canada," *Cultural Dynamics* 15, no. 3 (2003): 297.

27. Angela Fagerlin, Brian Zikmund-Fisher, Peter Ubel, "How Making a Risk Estimate Can Change the Feel of That Risk: Shifting Attitudes toward Breast Cancer Risk in a General Public Survey," *Patient Education and Counseling* 57, no. 3 (June 2005): 294–99; Penelope Hopwood, "Breast Cancer Risk Perception: What Do

We Know and Understand?" *Breast Cancer Research* 2 (2000): 387–91; Michelle Lobchuck, "Breast Cancer Risk Perception and Surveillance: An Investigative Review," *Online Journal of Knowledge Synthesis for Nursing* 10, no. 2 (May 2003); Lori Mosca and others, "Awareness, Perception, and Knowledge of Heart Disease Risk and Prevention among Women in the United States," *Archives of Family Medicine* 9 (June 9, 2000): 516–15; Sarah Wilcox and Marcia Stefanick, "Knowledge and Perceived Risk of Major Diseases in Middle-Aged and Older Women," *Health Psychology* 18 (1999): 346–53; Steven Woloshin and others, "Women's Perception of Breast Cancer Risk: How You Ask Matters," *Medical Decision Making* 19, no. 3 (July–September 1999): 221–29.

28. Lisa Duggan, *The Twilight of Equality? Neoliberalism, Cultural Politics, and the Attack on Democracy* (New York: Beacon Press, 2003), 70.

5. The Culture of Survivorship and the Tyranny of Cheerfulness

1. Audre Lorde, *The Cancer Journals* (San Francisco: Spinster's Ink, 1980).

2. Barbara Ehrenreich, "Welcome to Cancerland," *Harper's,* November 2001, 49.

3. Ibid., 50.

4. Ibid., 48, 50.

5. Ibid., 49.

6. Lorde, *Cancer Journals,* 74.

7. Ibid., 10.

8. Ibid., 74.

9. Ehrenreich, "Welcome to Cancerland," 48.

10. Paul Starr, *The Social Transformation of American Medicine: The Rise of a Sovereign Profession and the Making of a Vast Industry* (New York: Basic Books, 1982), 336.

11. Steven Epstein, *Impure Science: AIDS Activism and the Politics of Knowledge* (Berkeley: University of California Press, 1996).

12. Ibid., 13.

13. Max Navarre, "Fighting the Victim Label," in *AIDS: Cultural Analysis/Cultural Activism,* ed. Douglas Crimp (Cambridge: MIT Press, 1988), 143–67; Jan Zita Grover, "AIDS: Keywords," in *AIDS,* ed. Crimp, 17–30.

14. Navarre, "Fighting the Victim Label," 143.

15. Ibid., 144.

16. Ibid., 148.

17. Saba Bahar, "If I'm One of the Victims, Who Survives? Marilyn Hacker's Breast Cancer Texts," *Signs* 28, no. 4 (2003): 1025–52.

18. Laura Beil, "Life after Cancer," *Dallas Morning News,* April 6, 1998, sec. D, 7.

19. Ibid.

20. Epstein, *Impure Science,* 11.

21. Jennifer Myhre, "Medical Mavens: Gender, Science and the Consensus Politics of Breast Cancer Activism" (PhD diss., University of California, Davis, 2001).

22. Ulrike Boehmer, *The Personal and the Political: Women's Activism in Response to the Breast Cancer and AIDS Epidemics* (New York: SUNY Press, 2000); Amy Sue Bix, "Diseases Chasing Money and Power: Breast Cancer and AIDS Activism Challenging Authority," in *Health Care Policy in Contemporary America,* ed. Alan I. Marcus and Hamilton Cravens (University Park: Penn State University Press, 1997), 5–32; Patricia Kauffert, "Women, Resistance and the Breast Cancer Movement," in *Pragmatic Women and Body Politics,* ed. Margaret Lock and Patricia Kauffert (New York: Cambridge University Press, 1998), 287–309; Myhre, "Medical Mavens."

23. Kauffert, "Women, Resistance and the Breast Cancer Movement," 303.

24. Myhre, "Medical Mavens."

25. Duggan, *Twilight of Equality,* 68.

26. Cathy Cohen, *The Boundaries of Blackness: AIDS and the Breakdown of Black Politics* (Chicago: University of Chicago Press, 1999).

27. Boehmer, *Personal and Political;* Maren Klawiter, "From Private Stigma to Global Assembly: Transforming the Terrain of Breast Cancer," *Global Ethnography: Forces, Connections, and Imaginations in a Postmodern World,* ed. Michael Burawoy and others (Berkeley: University of California Press, 2000), 420–73.

28. Boehmer, *Personal and Political;* Myhre, "Medical Mavens."

29. Moffett, "Moving Beyond"; Myhre, "Medical Mavens"; Maren Klawiter, "Racing for the Cure, Walking Women, and Toxic Touring: Mapping Cultures of Action within the Bay Area Terrain of Breast Cancer," *Social Problems* 46, no. 1 (1999): 104–26.

30. John McCarthy and Mark Wolfson, "Consensus Movements, Conflict Movements and the Cooptation of Civic and State Infrastructures," in *Frontiers in Social Movement Theory,* ed. Aldon Morris and Carol Mueller (New Haven, Conn.: Yale University Press, 1992), 273–97; Myhre, "Medical Mavens."

31. Myhre, "Medical Mavens."

32. Langer, quoted in Debra Goldman, "Illness as a Metaphor," *Adweek,* November 3, 1997, 70; Jane Levere, "National Breast Cancer Awareness Month Has Inspired Extensive Corporate Advertising," *New York Times,* October 3, 1996, sec. D, 6.

33. Marita Sturken, *Tangled Memories: The Vietnam War, the AIDS Epidemic, and the Politics of Remembering* (Berkeley: University of California Press, 1997), 173.

34. Lorde, *Cancer* Journals, 73, 15, 10.

35. Ibid., 17.

36. Marie McCullough, "A Cancer Crusade Turns Contentious—Some Say the

Breast Cancer 'Industry' Has Become Too Much of a Good Thing," *Philadelphia Inquirer,* September 30, 2004.

37. Lorde, *Cancer Journals,* 45.

Conclusion

1. It will become clear as the discussion proceeds that some of the implications that relate specifically to the future of the battle against breast cancer are not solely or in some cases predominantly the result of the corporate model I have outlined in the book. But given the unfeasibility of disaggregating this model from the impact of grassroots activism, policy making, and so on, the discussion is designed as an attempt to capture as fully as possible those changes in which it has played some role. At the same time, I have excluded from my discussion those accomplishments—for instance, the inclusion of breast cancer advocates in the research process—that have had little, if anything, to do with the forces that form the focus of the book.

2. See chapter 4, n. 27.

3. Anne Kasper, "Barriers and Burdens: Poor Women Face Breast Cancer," in *Breast Cancer: Society Shapes an Epidemic,* ed. Anne Kasper and Susan Ferguson (New York: Palgrave, 2000), 183–212.

4. Ibid., 185.

5. Lauren Berlant, introduction to *Compassion: The Culture and Politics of an Emotion,* ed. Lauren Berlant (New York: Routledge, 2004), 2.

6. Breast Cancer Action, "The Puzzle Project: Background," http://www.bcaction.org/Pages/TakeAction/PPBackground.html.

7. Ibid.

8. Lisa Duggan, *The Twilight of Equality? Neoliberalism, Cultural Politics, and the Attack on Democracy* (New York: Beacon Press, 2003), 67, 68–69.

9. National Prostate Cancer Action Coalition, "Action Update Archives," http://www.pcacoalition.org/site/PageServer?pagename=advocacy_update_home.

10. Duggan, *Twilight of Equality,* 68.

11. Barbara Ehrenreich, "Welcome to Cancerland," *Harper's,* November 2001, 46.

Index

Samantha King is associate professor of kinesiology and health studies and women's studies at Queen's University, Kingston, Ontario. Her research on breast cancer, corporate philanthropy, and neoliberalism has appeared in *Social Text, International Journal of Qualitative Studies in Education,* and *International Journal of Sport Marketing and Sponsorship.* She has also published essays on the politics of health, sport, and the body in numerous edited collections and journals in the fields of cultural, critical race, and gender studies.